THE PAIN REPROCESSING THERAPY WORKBOOK FOR TEENS

REWIRE YOUR BRAIN TO FIND RELIEF FROM CHRONIC PAIN

DANIELLA DEUTSCH, LCSW
PENINA ZILBERBERG, PHD
PAULINA SOBLE, LCSW

Instant Help Books
An Imprint of New Harbinger Publications, Inc.

Publisher's Note

This publication is designed to provide accurate and authoritative information in regard to the subject matter covered. It is sold with the understanding that the publisher is not engaged in rendering psychological, financial, legal, or other professional services. If expert assistance or counseling is needed, the services of a competent professional should be sought.

New Harbinger Publications is an employee-owned company.

NATIONAL CENTER FOR EMPLOYEE OWNERSHIP NCEO MEMBER

Instant Help Books
An imprint of New Harbinger Publications, Inc.
5720 Shattuck Avenue
Oakland, CA 94609
www.newharbinger.com

Cover design by Amy Daniels

Illustrations by Aliza Zilberberg

Interior design by Tom Comitta

Acquired by Ryan Buresh

Edited by Karen Schader

Library of Congress Cataloging-in-Publication Data on file

MIX Paper | Supporting responsible forestry FSC® C008955 FSC www.fsc.org

Printed in the United States of America

28 27 26

10 9 8 7 6 5 4 3 2 1 First Printing

"*The Pain Reprocessing Therapy Workbook for Teens* is a fantastic resource! It is chock-full of the latest science about pain in an accessible and interesting format. It helps teens understand their own pain and provides a comprehensive guide for recovery. It should be the first book any teen with chronic pain reads!"

—**HOWARD SCHUBINER, MD,** clinical professor at the Michigan State University College of Human Medicine, and author of *Unlearn Your Pain*

"As someone who suffered from chronic pain from an early age, a resource like this would've been invaluable. Now, as a therapist specializing in neuroplastic symptoms, I confidently recommend it to my young patients. Packed with practical tools, creative activities, relatable language, engaging visuals, and a big dose of hope, it helps teens take charge and build confidence, resilience, and lasting relief. This workbook is a long-awaited, essential addition to the mind-body medicine landscape."

—**CHRISTIE UIPI, LCSW,** founder and executive director of The Better Mind Center

"Reading this workbook feels like having a smart, encouraging friend by your side. Someone who gets what it's like to be a teen living with chronic pain. The science is approachable and compelling, cleverly inviting curiosity over pressure. As a parent, I loved how the stories captured a teen's experience, while empowering them to recover. You'll feel understood and supported as you learn to trust your mind and body again."

—**CHARLIE MERRILL, MSPT,** mind-body physical therapist, athlete, content creator, and consultant

"I recently asked a crowded high school auditorium how many students experienced persistent pain—surprisingly, nearly every hand went up. Adolescent chronic pain is a hidden epidemic. This book meets that overwhelming need, giving young people a hopeful and practical road map to lasting relief."

—**JOHN GRIBBIN,** CEO of Curable Health

"Finally! A workbook that explains the new neuroscience of pain reprocessing therapy (PRT) to resolve chronic pain—in language that makes sense to teens. I've worked in clinics, hospitals and ICUs for thirty years. Medically unexplained pain is a very common problem that now has a solution. Parents, *buy this book!* Help your teen get back to the awesome human being that you know they really are."

—**BRAD FANESTIL, MD,** board-certified doctor of internal medicine at the Boulder Institute for Mind Body Medicine

"PRT is paradigm shifting. In data from my lab and my colleagues' labs, we are seeing people *recover* from chronic pain by understanding neuroplasticity and working to shift beliefs, behaviors, and emotions. This wonderful adaptation for teens offers a practical and compassionate path forward. Engaging exercises and guidance empowers teens—and those who support them—to understand, and change, their pain."

—**YONI K. ASHAR, PHD,** assistant professor at the University of Colorado Anschutz Medical Campus, and director at its Pain and Emotion Research Laboratory

DEDICATIONS

PENINA

To David:

Your selfless support, your unwavering belief in me and my ideas, and your daily ice coffees are the wind beneath my wings. It is because of you that I can do what I do.

To Rosie, Moshe, Aliza, and Ella:

Being your mom makes me happy every single day. Point blank period! You have shown me, as I hope I've shown you, that there is no such thing as can't.

DANIELLA

To my daughters, Lily, Arya, and Noa: You see, Mom might actually have some good ideas!

And to my dear husband, Isaac, who successfully convinced me that I did: Thank you for your love, support, and (relentless) encouragement.

PAULINA

To my son, Harrison: Being your mom is the greatest joy of my life.

To my husband, Oliver. Thank you for your unwavering support in all that I do. I wouldn't be me without you.

And to our sweetest girl, Lola: We adore you endlessly.

CONTENTS

FOREWORD

The authors have done a wonderful job synthesizing their knowledge and experience in treating chronic pain. Moreover, they present this in a comprehensive but comprehensible way for teenagers.

Teenagers, also known as adolescents, are a very important population in terms of chronic pain and neuroplastic symptoms. First, they are at a vulnerable age, with many emotional pressures, rapid bodily changes, and a maturing nervous system. Second, relief of pain at this age leads to more normal development and benefits them for more potential years than it does older adults. Finally, educating this population about this diagnosis and approach may lead to more societal awareness as they get better and age into their twenties and thirties.

Teenagers will become our future doctors, nurses, and psychotherapists. They will become our political leaders. Learning how to heal from pain and learning about the mind-body connection at this age is invaluable to their future awareness and maturation.

To the teenager that is opening this book: I have used this approach with thousands of adults and hundreds of teens. It really works. But it is different from a lot of medical treatments where the patient is more passive in the process. You really must dig in and play an active role to solve this pain puzzle. This workbook makes it easy to do so because it engages you with great questions, exercises, and clever cartoon figures and drawings. I am sure you want to get better. Using *The Pain Reprocessing Therapy Workbook for Teens* can really help you get your life back!

To parents and doctors: I know that this approach may be unfamiliar to many of you. It is extremely familiar to me, and I urge you to expose the affected teenager to this workbook.

Guidance and support can be challenging for teenagers and, ideally, they will grasp the method and do the work on their own. But an adult figure can be important in motivating them to try. Sometimes a reward for finishing can be helpful!

DAVID SCHECHTER, MD

Author of *Think Away Your Pain* and *The MindBody Workbook for Teens*

http://www.MindBodyMedicine.com

AN INTRODUCTION FOR PARENTS

Watching your teen struggle with chronic pain can be even more unbearable than facing pain yourself. It's exhausting and overwhelming, and it can feel like it's taken over every aspect of your life. We understand the journey you have been on, the toll it's taken on you physically, emotionally, financially, and relationally. Perhaps you've reached a point where you've put everything on hold—work, social outings, even your own self-care—to care for a child who's in too much pain to get out of bed. It can deplete the energy available for yourself, your intimate relationships, and your family. But perhaps the most challenging part is the helplessness—the fear that you cannot take away their pain, no matter how hard you try.

As parents, your instinct is to fix, protect, and do whatever it takes to ease your child's suffering. In an instant, you'd trade places with your child if it meant they could find relief and get their life back. You've likely gone from one doctor to another, pursuing tests and a diagnosis, clinging to the hope that someone, somewhere, has the solution. The hope is that a diagnosis, even a scary one, could at least offer a plan for recovery. If only a pill or surgery could be the cure. After all, doesn't physical pain mean there must be a physical problem that can be fixed with the proper physically targeted treatment? Shouldn't it be simple enough to locate the issue and solve it? The surprising and hopeful truth is that the answer lies elsewhere.

Of course, it is always important to first rule out any physical injury. But if test results do not support a physical diagnosis, or if your doctor has said that your child's pain cannot be fully explained by physical damage, infection, or injury, then pain reprocessing therapy (PRT) is the program for you and your teen. PRT is a set of psychological techniques aimed at teaching the brain to interpret and respond to sensations correctly, turning off faulty pain signals. We have written this PRT workbook with the research and practical experience in treating chronic pain and anxiety and explaining these concepts to kids and teens.

Chronic pain refers to pain lasting longer than three months. Interestingly, research shows most chronic pain is neuroplastic, which means the pain is not rooted in a physical problem but rather in the malfunctioning pain signaling in the brain and nervous system. Pain can begin with no injury at all. Other times, there is an initial injury or tissue damage, but the pain persists long after the normal course of healing—like a broken alarm clock that keeps ringing. This type of chronic pain isn't rooted in a bodily problem, which explains why searching for solely physical or medical solutions hasn't worked. Neuroplastic pain occurs when the brain's protective mechanisms go haywire, sending pain messages even when they're no longer needed.

It's understandable to feel confused by this. If there's no tissue damage, what is the explanation for your child's suffering? Is the pain even real? Let us assure you: your child's pain is very real. Neuroplastic pain doesn't mean your child is imagining their suffering or exaggerating their experience. Pain is protective and necessary for survival. But your child's brain is misinterpreting neutral sensory information as dangerous and reacting to perceived threat by ringing the alarm unnecessarily. Your teen's brain and pain-processing system are hypersensitive to sensations. But false alarms are just as loud as real ones. Whether pain begins with an injury; a condition like juvenile arthritis, fibromyalgia, or migraines; or even with no apparent issue (such as chronic headaches or stomach aches), the brain's misfiring pain signals, learned neural pathways, and predictive processing are at the core of the experience. How intense pain feels depends on how much danger the brain perceives based on what it has learned and its subsequent predictions. Understanding that chronic pain is rooted in the brain's faulty alarm system opens up an exciting opportunity: If the brain can learn to create pain, it can also unlearn it. Research has identified key factors that influence the brain's amplification or reduction of pain signals. This workbook will guide you and your teen to utilize the power of the brain to quiet these unnecessary signals.

Neuroplastic pain can be treated through intentional, science-backed strategies. The most encouraging news is that neuroplasticity, or the brain's incredible ability to learn and change, is especially strong during childhood and adolescence. In fact, a child's brain is highly adaptable and malleable through their early to mid-twenties, giving your teen the strongest capacity to rewire their brain and break free from the pain cycle.

One of the biggest factors fueling your child's pain is their belief and fear that something is wrong with their body. PRT tackles these beliefs and fears head-on to rewire the brain and turn off the false alarm. So, if you've been feeling fearful, hopeless, or helpless, try to put those feelings aside. How you respond to your child's pain and circumstance will greatly impact them in achieving their recovery goals.

THE GOALS OF THIS WORKBOOK

This workbook is a resource for your teen to work through independently, but you can also read alongside them as they process the information. You'll gain valuable insights into how chronic pain develops and persists and how to rewire the brain using PRT to achieve lasting relief. Together, you and your teen will work toward several key goals:

- **UNDERSTANDING PAIN.** Your teen will learn how the brain creates and amplifies pain, why fear and avoidance perpetuate the cycle, and how PRT can break that cycle.
- **REWIRING THE BRAIN TO REDUCE FEAR AND DEACTIVATE PAIN SIGNALS.** They'll explore practical strategies, such as breathing techniques, relaxation, mindfulness, somatic exercises, and more PRT techniques to manage triggers, regulate emotions, and reduce stress and pain.
- **GETTING BACK TO LIFE.** This workbook strategically and safely guides your teen to return to school, friends, activities, and sports.
- **FOSTERING INDEPENDENCE AND EMPOWERMENT.** When ready, your teen will expand their comfort zone and learn to trust their ability to manage pain, care for themselves, and advocate for their needs.

YOUR ROLE AS A PARENT IN THE RECOVERY PROCESS

As a parent, your role in your teen's recovery is critical—but not in the way you might expect. It's natural to want to swoop in and remove your child's pain. But panic and preoccupation with "fixing" the pain actually send the wrong message to their brain: that they are in danger, and need the pain—and you—to stay safe.

Your perception and belief are powerful. Kids and teens get their sense of how capable they are from what they think you think they can do. Your job will be to communicate that they are safe, that movement is not going to hurt them, and that they are capable of gradually returning to their life. While it may feel counterintuitive, encouraging your teen to return to their activities is a key part of retraining their brain.

As their parent, you have an essential role in striking the balance between offering compassion and encouraging independence. Teens with chronic pain often lean into the comfort of staying close to home and depending on their parents for reassurance. While this feels safe in the moment, it reinforces the belief that their body is damaged, which can lead to avoidance, fear, and an increase in pain.

PRACTICAL STEPS TO SUPPORT YOUR TEEN

A crucial part of your teen's recovery is creating a supportive environment, particularly as they navigate returning to school and other responsibilities. Collaborating with your teen and their trusted teacher(s), guidance counselor, or therapist can help ensure a gradual, manageable reentry plan that includes regular breaks or accommodations as needed, a school staff member your teen can turn to for support if they choose to, and a safe space where they can regroup during challenging moments.

Involving your teen in this planning process gives them ownership of their progress, knowing that they have a solid home base and the power to choose breaks or support when needed. Your confidence and reassurance will help your child embrace this new approach and alleviate fear. We are confident that your teen's pain can be treated, even if their symptoms have been around for a long time. By understanding and directly targeting the root cause of your child's pain—their brain—you can both reclaim your lives.

AN INTRODUCTION FOR TEENS

Welcome to *The Pain Reprocessing Therapy Workbook for Teens*. This workbook is your guide to understanding the relationship between your brain and body, the tricky process of chronic pain, and as you will soon see, the not-as-tricky process of getting out of it. The authors of this book are a combination of pain and psychology experts passionate about helping teens like you get out of pain and anxiety so that you can get back to doing the things you love!

What if this workbook holds the secrets to making your chronic pain decrease and even disappear? Using the pages ahead, you will unravel the mystery of your symptoms and learn techniques to take charge of your pain. Imagine what would be different if *you* could be in charge of raising or lowering the volume of your pain—not some doctor but you could be in charge of your recovery.

If you're reading this book, there's a good chance that you've been in pain for quite some time. You might feel hopeless, alone, worried, or frustrated that the pain won't stop. All of these feelings are normal, and you are not alone. There are 1.5 billion people in chronic pain (Lurie and Javaid 2024). That's one in every five individuals, and many of them share the same fears and emotions as you.

We realize that pain has been such a negative force in your life, but what if we told you that pain is not all bad? You would probably look puzzled and ask, "How on earth could pain possibly be good?" The answer is that pain has a powerful purpose: to keep your body safe from danger. Pain is protective. If you were to trip and break your ankle, the pain would stop you in your tracks, forcing you to get off that ankle immediately and seek help. The pain would protect you by preventing you from putting pressure on your ankle until it healed. Once you recover, the pain goes away, as it has completed its job. You can return to regular activities, school, friends, and life.

But what if pain continues after your injury heals? What if you still feel like you can't return to your routine? It turns out that pain can exist even in the absence of damage to the body. Science shows you can experience pain without injury or illness, or even after an injury heals. Pain becomes the main problem in those cases, rather than the physical injury or illness behind it.

All pain hurts, and all pain is real pain. Pain without an injury does not feel different from pain with an injury. In most chronic pain cases, no injury or physical problem is causing the pain—it's just a false alarm. But a false alarm is just as loud as a real one. When a false alarm first sounds, you don't immediately know there is no real danger. So your brain can create a danger signal (pain) that may keep you away from your friends and your life for no good reason! This false alarm pain is called neuroplastic pain.

Neuro means brain, and plastic means learning or changing. Neuroplastic pain is when the brain makes a learning error—it interprets a safe signal from the body as if it were dangerous and learns to make that same misinterpretation repeatedly. We have learned from MRI images that pain from an injury lights up the somatosensory cortex, which is the part of the brain involved in sensing touch, temperature, and pain. Interestingly, chronic pain, or pain lasting longer than three months, activates a completely different area of the brain, the prefrontal cortex, which is involved in learning, memories, and judgment (Kross et al. 2011). We'll get into that more in later chapters, but the takeaway is that chronic pain is not the same as the pain you experience when you suffer an acute injury, like stubbing your toe or touching a hot oven, even though it feels like it is. Because chronic pain activates different brain regions, we must treat it differently.

Throughout this workbook, we will refer to fear and how it has been keeping you in chronic pain. Once the brain makes a misinterpretation, resulting in neuroplastic pain, you likely fear that something is wrong with your body. When the brain perceives threat, it continues to fire pain signals, keeping you in a cycle of persistent pain and fear. Fear can include many things—fear of bodily damage, fear of more pain, fear of not being able to manage high pain spikes, and more.

This workbook aims to help you decrease your fear around bodily sensations and use PRT to rewire your brain and interpret sensations accurately. Since your brain learned to create neuroplastic pain, it can also unlearn it. You are the driving force behind your healing. We'll be here with you, teaching, supporting, and rooting for you, but you'll be in charge. Are you ready to take your power back?

GETTING TO KNOW YOU AND YOUR PAIN

If you picked up this workbook, chances are you have been in pain for quite some time, visited countless doctors, and tried various tests and treatments. Doctors and experts may not have been able to find a physical explanation, and you've likely spent countless hours trying to figure out what is going on with your body and how to get rid of your pain. You want your pain-free life back, but nothing you've tried has resulted in lasting relief. Being in constant pain is so difficult and lonely, and you may feel helpless at times. Pain is exhausting; it can take away your energy and motivation pretty quickly. So, if you are here with us now, you have already taken the biggest step toward recovery. We'll soon explain how this program treats pain differently and why it will work for you.

But first, let's get to know you. Sometimes, pain takes over how you think about yourself and the things around you. Pain can make it hard to concentrate on anything else. Can you describe who you are—your pre-pain self? Below are some questions for you to consider about yourself unrelated to your pain. It might be challenging for you to remember, but try your best.

ACTIVITY GETTING TO KNOW YOUR PRE-PAIN SELF

What are three adjectives a friend would use to describe you?

1. ______
2. ______
3. ______

What are three adjectives you would use to describe yourself?

1. ______
2. ______
3. ______

List three things you like about yourself or are good at.

1. ______
2. ______
3. ______

On a scale of 1 (least challenging) to 5 (most challenging), how challenging was it to think of these positive traits?

______

List three things that make you nervous or afraid that are unrelated to your pain.

1. ______
2. ______
3. ______

What has made you feel strong and confident in yourself?

What is the bravest thing you remember doing?

Name three people in your life whom you trust and rely on:

1.
2.
3.

Close your eyes and imagine a happy place that makes you feel calm, relaxed, and secure. Where are you?

Now that we know who you are apart from the pain, has pain changed the way you think about yourself? Explain how.

Now, let's get a sense of how much your pain is taking over your life and preventing you from doing the things you would normally do.

ACTIVITY GETTING TO KNOW YOUR PAIN

Complete the following chart by placing a check mark in the column that best describes your belief:

BELIEF	STRONGLY DISAGREE	DISAGREE	AGREE	STRONGLY AGREE
I'm afraid that I might injure myself if I exercise.				
If I were to try to push myself, my pain would increase.				
My body is telling me there is something dangerously wrong.				
People aren't taking my medical condition seriously enough.				
My accident/injury/problem has put my body at risk for the rest of my life.				
Pain always means I have injured my body.				
Being careful to not make any unnecessary movements is the safest thing I can do to prevent my pain from worsening.				
I wouldn't have this much pain if there weren't something dangerous going on in my body.				
Pain lets me know when to stop exercising so that I don't injure myself.				
I can't do all the things normal people do because I will get injured.				

 Questions adapted from the Tampa Scale for Kinesiophobia (TSK-11 scale) (Woby et al., 2005).

WHY THIS APPROACH WORKS

You might be wondering how a workbook can help if doctors couldn't. It makes sense to question that. Feeling nervous or skeptical is a good thing—even a strength! Skepticism shows that you care about yourself and want to protect yourself from harm. After all, your other attempts to get better have ended in disappointment.

So, what's different about this workbook? Classic pain treatments focus on the injury behind the pain and how to accept and live with it. But if you have neuroplastic pain, and there is no injury or tissue damage, you *can* and *will* live your life without pain.

How you feel and think about your pain, what is causing it, and what you believe will help you get better are key to your recovery. Before starting PRT, many people believe their pain is caused by a physical injury and, therefore, needs a physical treatment to get better. That makes a lot of sense. The brain is hardwired to believe that physical pain means physical damage. However, if a physical injury is not causing your pain, physical interventions will not work. So, your pain has stuck around because you are not targeting the right issue. Using physical treatments for neuroplastic pain is like using antibiotics to treat a virus. Antibiotics won't work because they treat bacterial infections, not viral infections. Just as you would need the correct medicine to treat a specific infection, you need the right treatment for your specific pain.

This workbook and PRT target the root of neuroplastic pain: your brain. This is not to say your pain isn't real or that it is all in your head. In fact, everything you feel and perceive comes from your brain.

Take this illusion: **What do you see as you look directly at the black spot?**

The black spot is expanding, right?

It turns out it is not moving at all! But when your brain sees the dark spot, it expects that you're about to go into a dark room. Your pupils dilate to help you adapt to this environment. Your brain does this to keep you safe by helping you see in the dark.

Your pain is real, just like the phenomenon of your pupils dilating is real. But in both cases, there is no threat. Your brain simply made a mistake.

Why does this happen? The brain's primary job is ensuring your survival. It carries out this job by instantaneously deciding what is happening and predicting what might happen next. Usually, the brain does this well, but when sensory information isn't clear, the brain will compensate for missing information by "completing" it in a logical way. **For example, what do you see in this image?**

Although you probably see a triangle, there is no actual triangle drawn here. This image consists only of three black Pac-Mans, and your brain fills in a white triangle based on what it expects to see or what makes sense to you.

Here is another example of an illusion. **Which line looks longer?**

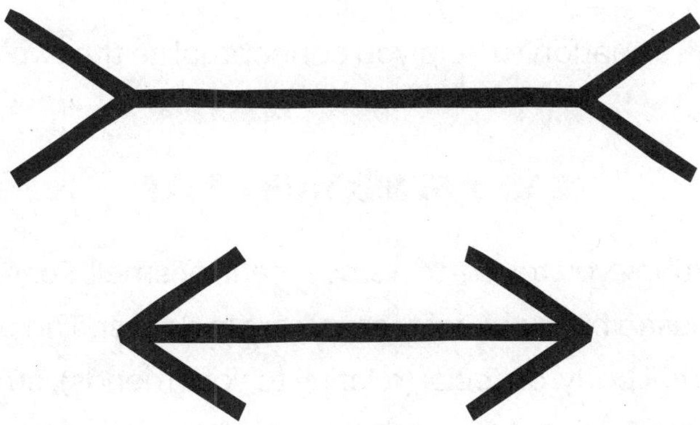

The illusion makes it look like the lines are different lengths, but they are actually identical. This happens because one line has arrow tails (fins pointing out), and the other has arrowheads (fins pointing in). The tails make your brain interpret the line as longer, while the arrowheads make your brain interpret the line as shorter.

Try it for yourself at home. Take two pipe cleaners, two strings, or two raw pieces of spaghetti of the same length and put one above the other, just like in this image. On one of the lines, put two smaller pieces as the fins pointing outward, and on the other line, put two smaller pieces as the fins pointing inward. As you can see, the line with the fins pointing outward will appear longer.

With all these images, your brain fills in or "sees" things in error. Since the brain's primary job is safety, it sometimes simplifies by erring on the side of caution. While this works for basic survival, and even for illusions, it does not work for neuroplastic pain. In this case, the brain's prediction and misinterpretation of sensory information is unhelpful. While mistakes happen, with neuroplastic pain, the mistake keeps happening over and over again, causing a chronic problem.

WHAT IS CHRONIC PAIN?

The widely accepted definition of pain is "an unpleasant sensory and emotional experience" (Raja et al. 2020). Pain becomes chronic when it lasts for over three months. Both physical and emotional factors contribute to the development of chronic pain. The treatment plan laid out in this workbook applies to any unpleasant sensory experience, including pain, fatigue, itchiness, dizziness, nausea, insomnia, and more.

Let's start with a simple equation to help you conceptualize the two experiences at play when you feel pain.

PAIN = SENSATION + FEAR

Sensation refers to anything you touch, taste, see, hear, or smell. Fear refers to any unpleasant emotion caused by the belief that you are in danger. The perceived danger can be related to your physical body, or social (relating to your friends), emotional (something you're worried about), or situational (something stressful in your environment) factors.

Fear is a pretty broad term. Some people say, "I am not afraid of my pain; I am just annoyed that it's still here!" There are many emotions that can fall under the umbrella of fear, including stress, anxiety, frustration, annoyance, hopelessness, worry, preoccupation, and feeling overwhelmed, to name a few.

Together, we will address all the fears that may contribute to the continuation of your pain. To start, let's divide your fears into two categories...or umbrellas!

What would you add to your personal umbrellas? **Fill your fears into the panels.**

Great job! Soon, we will explore how all these physical, social, emotional, and situational fears are keeping your neuroplastic pain alive.

BECOMING A PAIN DETECTIVE

But how do you know if you have neuroplastic pain? How do you know if this approach will work for you?

You will become a pain detective and gather clues to determine the root cause of your pain. Below are some of the questions we ask everyone who enters our office. Take some time now to respond and begin to unravel your case.

ACTIVITY BODY MAP

Where do you feel your symptoms? **On the body map below, mark the areas where you sometimes feel pain or discomfort.** Use whatever works for you—colors, drawings, words, or symbols—to show how it feels. For example, you might draw a gray spiral around the head to show dizziness, a red wavy line on the neck for soreness, or black butterflies in the stomach for discomfort.

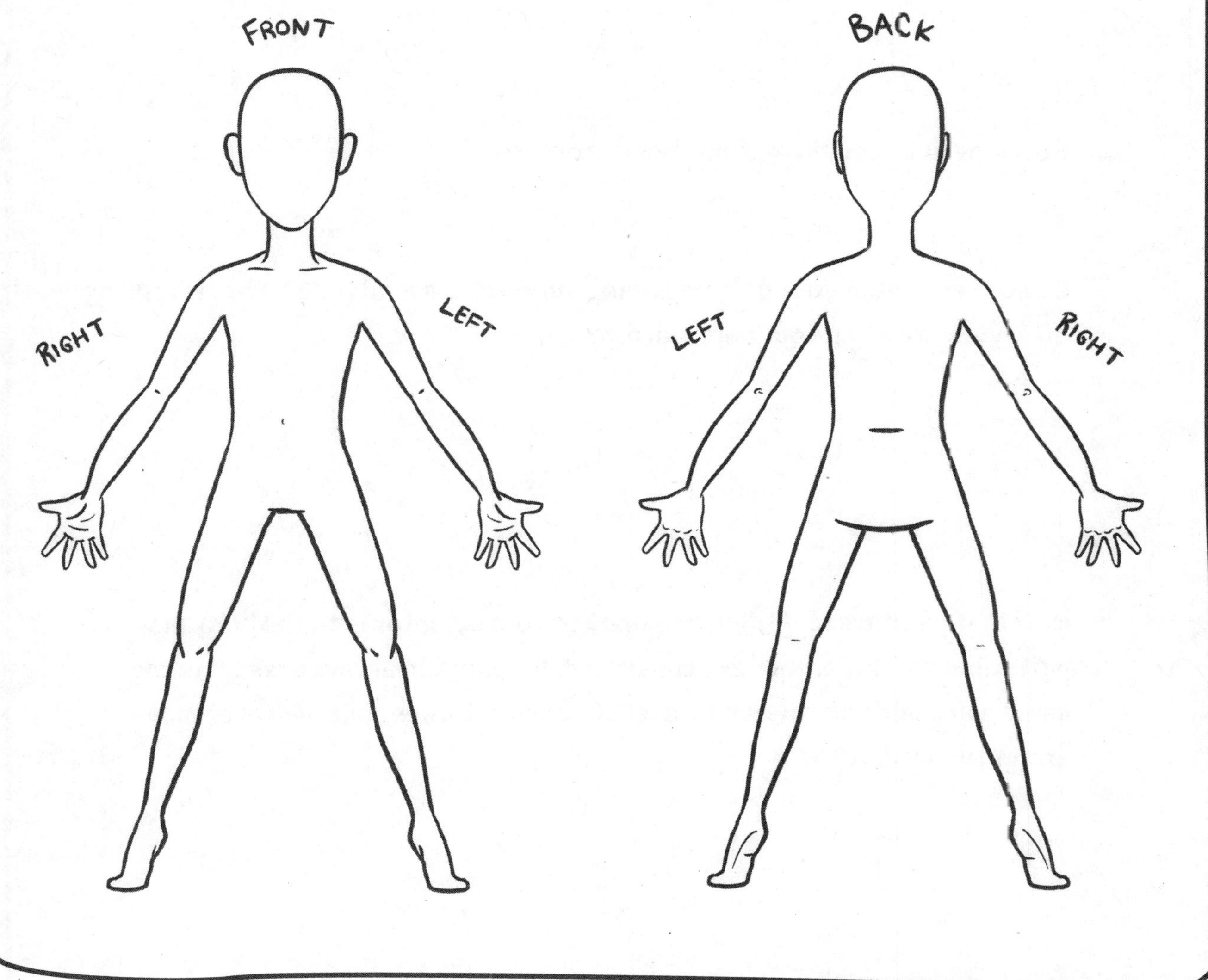

ACTIVITY INVESTIGATING YOUR SYMPTOMS

Now take some time to respond to the questions that follow.

1. **Did your pain begin with an injury? If so, how long ago was your injury? How long did doctors say it would take to heal from this injury?**

2. **How long have your symptoms been around?**

3. **Do you remember your pain beginning during a stressful time? What was going on in your life when your pain started?**

4. **Now that you have identified and marked your symptoms on the body map, write about whether they are consistent. Is your pain always present in the same place and with the same level of intensity? Does your pain ever move around your body?**

5. **When does your pain usually come on? Do you notice pain spiking after, but not during, an activity or movement?**

6. **What have doctors said is the cause of your pain? Do you have a diagnosis? Do you agree with their explanation?**

7. **If you have pain in multiple parts of your body now, or have in the past, describe them here:**

8. **What triggers your pain? Is your pain higher when you are stressed, tired, or agitated? When are your symptoms the worst?**

9. **What helps your pain? Do you notice your pain when you are doing something you enjoy?**

10. **What do your parents think is the cause of your pain? What do they say to do when you are in pain? Do you feel they understand what you are dealing with?**

11. **Do you identify as a perfectionist? A people pleaser? Are you often anxious? Do you tend to put others' needs before your own? Explain your response.**

12. **Does anyone else in your family deal with chronic pain? If so, describe their pain, including when and how often they get it, and how they manage it. Does it stop them from doing their work or fulfilling responsibilities?**

A PEEK BEHIND THE CURTAIN: WHY WE ASKED AND WHAT YOUR ANSWERS REVEAL

All of the questions you just answered can help you gather clues to figure out if you have neuroplastic pain.

1. If your pain began without an injury, that's a sign that it's neuroplastic. But even if your pain started with an injury, injuries heal. If pain continues long after an injury happened, it's likely neuroplastic as well.

2. Pain that persists for over three months is considered chronic. Studies show that most chronic pain does not have a physical explanation (Baliki et al. 2012). In fact, a study conducted on 222 chronic pain patients determined that pain was unrelated to physical damage in 88 percent of patients (Schubiner et al. 2023).

3. Stress falls under the umbrella of fear. Stress can cause irritability and overall sensitivity, triggering neuroplastic pain.

4. If you break your ankle, every time you step on it, it will hurt in the same place. Pain from a physical injury doesn't move around, come and go, or act inconsistently. Pain that moves from one part of the body to another is a clue that you may have neuroplastic pain.

5. Pain from an injury often occurs while exercising or applying pressure to the body. Neuroplastic pain sometimes appears long after an activity has finished, indicating that the brain may have a significant role in the pain experience.

6. If doctors cannot find a clear cause for your pain, that's a solid clue that it is neuroplastic. But even with a diagnosis, your pain may still be neuroplastic. Some diagnoses describe your symptoms but do not identify a physical cause for them.

7. Having three or four unrelated medical conditions is quite unlikely. Specifically, if pain pops up in different areas of your body simultaneously, it is doubtful

that it is from tissue damage, injury, or illness. A single underlying cause—your brain's mistake—is much more likely.

8. Sometimes, pain becomes linked with specific activities, smells, sounds, light, the time of day, or the weather. When pain triggers have nothing to do with your body, the pain is likely neuroplastic.
9. Are you aware of your pain when you're engaged in something you enjoy? If you do not notice your pain as much when watching your favorite TV show or sports game, your brain's influence may be at play.
10. Not feeling heard or understood can trigger negative emotions or make you feel less safe. And anything that makes you feel unsafe can trigger neuroplastic pain.
11. All these traits put the brain on high alert, signaling danger to your brain.
12. A family member dealing with chronic pain can make you believe you are more vulnerable to developing it yourself due to biology and genetics. But just because your family member has a chronic issue does not mean that it is genetic or that you are destined to get it too.

After reviewing these clues, are you starting to suspect your pain might be neuroplastic? These clues are meant to help you gather evidence and determine what is causing your pain. Your symptoms don't need to meet all the above criteria to be neuroplastic. In fact, your pain may be neuroplastic even if you meet only one. That would certainly explain why physical treatments have not been enough to get rid of your pain.

Discovering that you can eliminate your pain by retraining your brain might be a relief. But at this stage, it's okay to remain skeptical. You probably will believe this explanation with certainty only once you're out of pain. Keep reading to learn how the brain affects your perceptions and feelings and how this relates to your pain.

In this chapter, you reflected on your pre-pain self, including how you think and feel about your pain symptoms. You also learned about the relationship between pain and the brain:

- How the brain can get tricked into perceiving things that aren't there
- How with chronic pain, there is often no injury
- That physical interventions will not work if there is no physical injury
- That proper treatment needs to target the cause of neuroplastic pain—the brain
- That neuroplastic pain is mistakenly created by the brain when there is no injury
- That pain becomes chronic when the brain's mistake or "false alarm" persists for longer than three months
- That pain = sensation + fear
- That fear umbrellas include fear of the pain and other fears that can influence pain
- How you can gather clues to help determine whether you have neuroplastic pain

THE AMAZING BODY-BRAIN CONNECTION

In the last chapter, you started to see that your perceptions and expectations can impact your pain experience. But how? Pain is the brain's form of communication. How would you communicate with your friend if they were about to get hit by a bus? You might scream really loudly so they know to jump out of the way. In the same way, pain is the brain's "scream" that urges you to react appropriately to a potential threat. Let's explore your brain-body connection and how you can go from simply feeling a sensation to springing into action.

THE BRAIN AND BODY WORK TOGETHER

Your brain and body typically work together smoothly like synchronized Olympic swimmers. Your brain is your control center—it receives messages from your body and the world around you. Based on this information, your brain decides the best course of action and then sends a message to your body, telling it what to do so you stay safe.

As you now know, pain is necessary for your survival. In fact, there's a rare and dangerous medical condition that prevents people from feeling pain, which unsurprisingly leads to a shorter life expectancy. That's because without pain, you would have no signal to notify you of a possible threat or injury. To demonstrate this, here's a quick story.

ELLA'S STORY: PAIN IS NOT ALL BAD

Ella is a conscientious student who loves going to school. She woke up one morning with intense stomach pains. Her mom made her a light toast and tea and told her to stay in bed. By the afternoon, her stomach pain was so excruciating that she could barely stand. She called her mom at work, saying that this pain was different from any she'd ever experienced. Her mom calmly instructed her to rest and added that it would surely pass. But Ella's pain was intense and unusual, indicating something was not right. Ella urged her mom, "Mom, this really, really hurts. I've got to see the doctor right away!"

Her mom left work early to take her. Thankfully she did, because the doctor immediately diagnosed Ella with appendicitis. Ella's mom rushed her to the emergency room, where the doctors confirmed the diagnosis and performed an emergency appendectomy.

If not for the strength of Ella's pain—the intense signal her brain sent her—her appendix could have ruptured and caused a severe infection. You see, pain is not all bad—it's actually necessary when there is danger.

Can you remember a time when a strong sensation or pain kept you safe from danger? What was the situation, what did you feel, and how did you respond? How did that pain keep you safe or prevent further injury?

Pain is a danger signal. If your appendix ruptured and you felt no pain, you would not get life-saving medical treatment. In the same way, if you touched a hot oven but felt no pain, you would not know to remove your hand, causing further damage. These pain signals are necessary for survival.

The problem is that the brain sometimes makes mistakes, sending pain signals when there is no injury or danger. In that case, your pain is an error, needlessly keeping you in danger mode (and in pain).

NEUROPLASTIC PAIN: WHAT IS LEARNED CAN BE UNLEARNED

Neuroplastic pain happens when the brain interprets safe signals from the body as if they were dangerous and responds by creating feelings of pain. The good news is that, just as your brain can learn pain, it can also unlearn it. The even better news is that the brains of kids and teens are more plastic and flexible than those of adults, making it even easier and faster to unlearn pain.

First, you will learn to identify the difference between pain due to real danger and pain that is simply the brain's mistake. Then, you will learn how to fix that error and regain your pain-free life using PRT and other relaxation and behavioral techniques. PRT is a collection of tools that retrain your brain to interpret and respond to body signals correctly so that you can differentiate between threat and safety. In this way, when you are safe, your brain will no longer mistakenly send pain signals, and you will reduce and even eliminate your chronic neuroplastic pain.

SENSING THE WORLD AROUND US

The first step is to learn how your brain receives messages from your body. You gain information through your five senses (sight, smell, sound, taste, and touch), and you begin to use these senses from the first moment you wake up each morning. You open your eyes and may find all the comforting things in your room: the soft pillow behind your head, your fleece throw blanket, and the familiar color of your wall. You might feel content and excited for the day ahead if you look outside your window and see a blue sky and a bright shining sun.

If, on another day, you look outside and see snow falling, how will that make you feel? That depends on your situation. If you've been hoping for a day off from school, you may feel relieved and enthusiastic. But for an adult with an early morning meeting at work, the snow on the ground may not evoke enthusiasm. It might cause worry about getting the car out of the driveway and making it to the destination safely. So you can already see a bit about how context may impact the brain's decision about what your eyes just saw.

Have you ever woken up disoriented and unsure if you need to rush out of bed to make your ride to school? You might open your eyes and take a moment to figure it out. Without realizing it, your senses are quickly sending information to your brain. Let's take a look at how this happens.

ANTHONY'S STORY: THE BRAIN-BODY CONNECTION

Anthony awoke with a startle and looked directly at his phone. It was 8:30! He suddenly felt panicked and noticed his heart was racing. He was annoyed that his siblings had left for school without him and nervous about missing class. Questions spiraled in his mind...*How am I going to get to school? Why didn't my alarm go off? Why didn't anyone wake me up?* He strained to listen for sounds coming from the kitchen. He heard the coffee pot bubbling, dishes rattling, and the sound of the morning news. He breathed in the smell of fresh pancakes. Instantly, he remembered that in his house, fresh pancakes are strictly for Sunday mornings when no one is rushing to work! Anthony breathed a sigh of relief, realizing that he was not late for school. His heartbeat regulated and he sank back into his pillow. Based on the incoming information—what he saw, smelled, and heard—his brain swiftly informed him that there was no threat and that he didn't need to panic or rush.

Your senses constantly send messages to your brain. Then, your brain instantly decides if you are safe, comfortable, in danger, or need to hurry. In a flash, your brain tells your body what it must do. This is the brain-body connection.

HOW DOES THE BRAIN CREATE PAIN?

As you just read, your brain constantly takes in information from your senses, assesses what is happening, and decides what you need to do. Sometimes, your brain detects a threat to your body and sends a pain message to protect you. Everyone feels pain from time to time—it means that you are paying attention to the world around you and that your brain is doing everything it can to keep you safe and healthy.

Pain is an unpleasant sensory and emotional experience. Sensory refers to anything your body takes in through your senses—anything you see, hear, touch, smell, or taste. Emotional refers to how you feel about a situation; are you happy, sad, angry, worried, scared, or excited? Your emotional experience includes what you are paying attention to, thinking, remembering, and expecting. For example, imagine someone gave you a ripe peach. If you were expecting an apple, the peach might taste rotten. But if you were expecting a peach, it would probably taste delicious. So your experience of the peach depends on your expectation.

Your experience of pain is quite similar in that it also depends on your emotions and expectations. Earlier, we introduced the equation that Pain = Sensation + Fear. Here's an equation that explores this concept further.

Pain includes both the sensory experience (what you feel, smell, taste, see, or hear) and the emotional experience (what you think, expect, believe, remember, and the mood you are in).

When you feel pain, a team of players in your body work together to create that sensation. Imagine hopping into a steaming hot shower after a long school day without checking the water temperature. Your skin will immediately take cues from your environment through touch. Your skin will feel the hot water and send a message to your brain like "Danger felt on the skin of your back!" Your brain will instantly decide whether there is a threat and create a pain message to warn you if there is. If that pain message is strong, it will push you to jump out of the shower or quickly regulate the faucet to prevent further harm.

But your pain level can also change depending on other things, like your mood, what you're doing, or the things around you. For example, imagine you prick your finger while hanging out with friends. You might not notice the pain because you're having fun. Now suppose you prick that finger while a rabid dog is chasing you. In this case, you may not feel the pain either because your brain needs to focus on running away, not on your finger. But suppose you prick that finger while upset about an argument with one of your siblings. The pain may feel much more intense because of your mood.

Can you think of a time when you didn't realize you were hurt because you were distracted by something else? Describe the situation. Where were you hurt, and what distracted you from that pain? When did you realize that you were injured?

Your brain acts like an emergency room nurse deciding who needs medical attention first. Imagine you are the nurse in charge, and three patients are trying to get medical attention—one has a fever and cough, the second has a broken ankle, and the third has a head injury.

Circle the patient you would admit first:

PATIENT 1: FEVER AND COUGH

PATIENT 2: BROKEN ANKLE

PATIENT 3: HEAD INJURY

If you chose patient 3, you are correct! The patient with the head injury would require the most immediate attention.

Your brain is responsible for doing the same thing—giving its attention to the greatest potential danger. Knowing how the brain works is very helpful, because you can actually shift your brain's attention to turn down your pain!

YOUR POWER TO TURN DOWN THE PAIN VOLUME

The pain you have been feeling might be intense, and it doesn't always feel like it is in your control. You can, however, learn how to raise or lower the intensity. How strongly you feel pain and how long your pain lasts is affected by how you're feeling, what you're paying attention to, and what your brain is thinking or telling you. You do have some power to raise or lower your pain intensity. It's almost like you hold a remote that you can turn up to make the pain louder or turn down to make it softer.

These things turn up the pain volume:

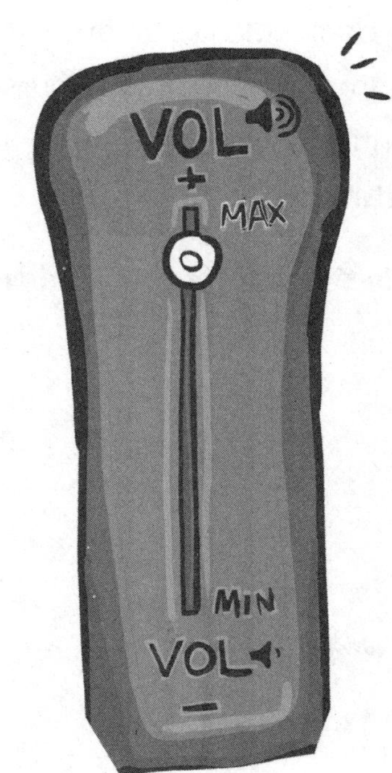

- Worrying about the pain coming back
- Believing that the pain is dangerous
- Feeling stressed
- Not getting enough sleep

To demonstrate this, let's take a look at Sam:

Sam was experiencing frequent migraines and back pain. He noticed that his pain wasn't consistent (remember, this is one of the neuroplastic pain clues revealed in chapter 1). Sometimes, Sam's pain would disappear for a few hours, but then it would come back with a vengeance. He noticed that his pain would fluctuate based on his stress level. So, he decided to make a list of pain triggers. His list included:

- Thinking about missing school work because of my pain
- Studying for the SATs
- Speaking with my dad about going to college out of state
- Overhearing my parents arguing about money

Sam's list helped him recognize the social, emotional, and situational fears that impacted his mood and his pain. When you're aware, it's easier to bear. In later chapters, you'll learn to use this knowledge to help you better manage your stress, which will also alleviate your pain.

What are some specific things that turn up your pain volume? Write them here:

The brain sends a pain signal when it believes you are in danger, for a variety of reasons. Perhaps the reasons include worry about pain, or worry about a big test you have tomorrow. Thoughts, beliefs, and feelings can trigger the brain's danger detector. In other words, when you think of upsetting thoughts or feel anxious or afraid, you unintentionally increase the pain intensity. For example, suppose you were feeling stressed and overwhelmed. In that case, your brain would likely send stronger pain signals than if you were thinking *I am safe* or *I am going to be okay*. The good news is that because your brain can create and increase feelings of pain, you can also use your brain to help reduce or even eliminate pain with the right tools.

These things turn down the pain volume:

- Doing things that you enjoy
- Doing things that relax your body
- Telling yourself you'll be okay even if you feel some pain

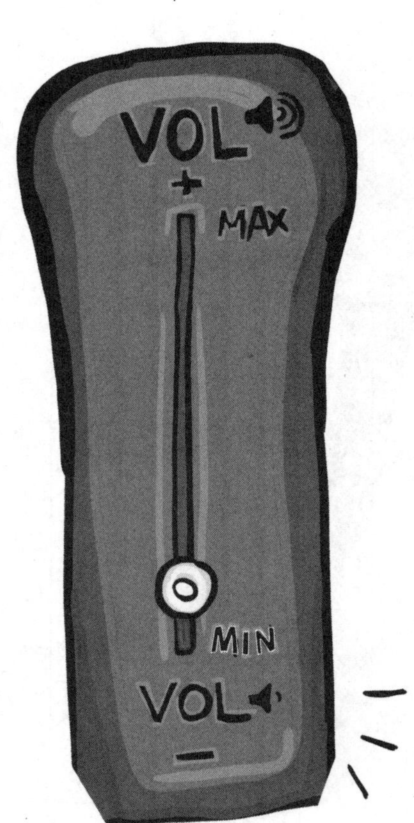

Sam started working with a therapist to take charge of his pain. His therapist suggested that he make a list of things that usually turn down the volume or intensity of his pain. His list included:

- Watching a tennis match on TV
- Playing my guitar
- Watching a movie with my girlfriend
- Playing fantasy football with my friends

What puts you in a good mood or makes your pain quieter? Write your list here:

Things that make my pain QUIETER:

1.

2.

3.

4.

5.

6.

7.

8.

9.

10.

11.

12.

QUESTIONS TO PONDER

Looking at the lists you just made for increasing and decreasing your pain volume, describe any patterns you notice.

Describe any specific moods that raise or lower your pain.

Think about the last time you were in pain. **Looking back at the list you made, describe anything you could use to address your mood and lower your pain.**

In this chapter, you learned about the ways that your brain and body work together to protect you, including:

- How the brain receives messages about the world around you from your body and your five senses
- How your brain uses incoming sensory information to send a message to your body, telling it what to do so you stay safe
- That pain is a brain signal notifying you of a possible threat or injury
- That the brain can sometimes make mistakes, sending pain signals when there is no injury or danger
- How neuroplastic pain happens when the brain interprets safe signals from the body as if they were dangerous and responds by creating feelings of pain
- That just as your brain can learn pain, it can unlearn it
- That pain = sensory experience + emotional experience
- How your level of pain depends on your mood, emotions, expectations, and attention
- That you hold the power to turn your pain volume up or down

THE BRILLIANT BRAIN: YOUR BODY'S CONTROL CENTER

In the last chapter, you started to learn that the brain and body work together to interpret incoming signals and information. You also began to discover how your sensations interact with your feelings and expectations to create pain and keep you safe. In this chapter, the brain will be the main character. You will deepen your understanding of the mind-body connection and learn how the brain decides to send distress signals to your body, sometimes in the form of pain.

THE BRAIN IS BOSS: OUR SENSES AND BEYOND

In your family, your mom, dad, or another guardian might be the boss. That adult in charge of your family makes sure that everyone has what they need. Another kind of boss is the head or CEO of a big company. The CEO's job is to oversee every department and ensure that each part of the company is doing its job and working together efficiently. Your brain is your body's boss whose main job is to keep you safe and keep your body in balance.

The brain is the control center, receiving and interpreting information from your sense organs (your eyes, ears, nose, mouth, and skin). The brain then sends instructions to every function your body engages in, like breathing, balance, learning, memory, and food digestion. The brain has different parts, each with its unique purpose. For example, a part of your brain called the hypothalamus regulates your body temperature to keep it stable.

When you're feeling cold, your hypothalamus signals your body to shiver to warm you up. When you're too hot, your hypothalamus signals your body to sweat to cool you off.

Think of a time when you felt hot and sweaty, then circle any of these situations that resonate:

Going to a school dance

Giving a presentation

Playing sports

Talking to your crush

Joining a conversation

Sitting out at the beach

Initiating plans

Teacher calling on you

Staying home alone

Taking a test

Add your own: ______________________________

In each of the above situations, the brain uses incoming sensory information to make a decision about your safety and notify your body how to respond. For example, if you feel hot, your brain will "look" around and decide if that sensation is because you are sitting out at a beach, coming down with a fever, or taking a test. When the brain assesses for threat, it combines the sensory cues with other information in your environment, like where you are and what you're doing, to decide what to communicate to your body. Your brain decides if you should move under an umbrella because the sun is too strong, grab a thermometer to check your temperature, or simply stay where you are because there is no imminent threat. Once your brain decides what is happening and how you should respond, it communicates with your body so that you know if action is needed.

THE BRAIN'S TINY MESSENGERS

As your body's control center, the brain quickly coordinates the transmission of information between your body and brain. In fact, the brain can receive and send messages faster than 100 miles per hour (Susuki 2010).

Your brain houses tiny cells called neurons.

These are tiny messengers sending and receiving sensory information between the brain, spinal cord, and body.

Let's take a look at how this plays out in action. Imagine that a bug lands on your foot. Sensory neurons in your skin send this information to your brain at lightning speed. Your brain then uses motor neurons to send that message back through your spinal cord to your foot to shake the bug off immediately. That's another example of your brain acting as the control center to keep you safe.

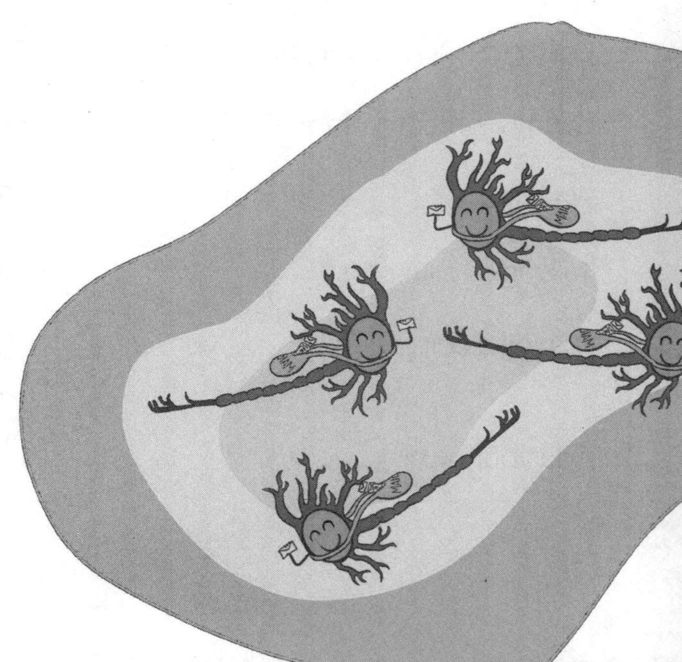

THE BRAIN AND PAIN

Any time your brain senses something that might be dangerous, it sends a message to your body to keep you safe. Just like it sends you a message to move your foot to get the bug off so that it can't hurt you, the brain will send a message to move your hand off a hot stove or get out of a steaming hot shower!

The brain will even send a message to your body to run away when it thinks you are in danger. When your brain detects potential danger, it may produce fear and send all your body's energy to your legs and feet so you can run away.

THE BRAIN HAS THE FINAL SAY

The brain's signals provide important information about your body and environment. Sometimes signals can be whispers, like a slight discomfort, and other times, they can be loud alarms, like a sharp pain. Paying attention helps you become a skilled detective in decoding what your body is trying to tell you.

What sensory signals indicate danger? How might your brain interpret those signals? What will your brain instruct your body to do based on this interpretation? Can you come up with some others signals you might see, hear, smell, or feel? Then, identify what the brain's decision and instructions to your body might be and add them to this chart. We've completed the first row to give you an example.

SENSORY SIGN (SEE, HEAR, SMELL, FEEL)	BRAIN'S DECISION	BRAIN'S INSTRUCTIONS TO BODY
Smell of smoke	There's a fire!	RUN!
Sound of school bell		
Sight of blood on your knee		

NEURAL PATHWAYS: PRACTICE MAKES PERFECT

Let's take it a step further. For the brain to act quickly and efficiently, it creates pathways, or connections. Every time you learn something new, your brain will create a new neural pathway containing tiny connecting neurons for that specific piece of information.

Think back to the first time you learned to type. If you ever watched someone typing before you knew how, you probably wondered, *How can they do that without even looking at the keyboard?* When you first started, you might have had to memorize where all the keys were, and it might have felt overwhelming, like you'd never remember them all. At first, you had to focus on where to place your hands, trying not to mess up and constantly check to ensure you weren't typing a bunch of gibberish. But after practicing, it became easier. Now, you can confidently sit at your computer, tablet, or phone, and your fingers automatically know where to go without even thinking about it.

Learning to play the piano works in a similar way. If you've ever seen a professional pianist play, you might have been amazed by how fast their fingers fly across the keys. But they didn't start off like that. The first step is learning the notes in a single octave, where they are on the instrument, and what each note sounds like. Then, you learn how the notes look on sheet music, so you can quickly spot a C, D, E, F, G, A, or B and find it on the piano. With practice, this process becomes smoother and faster until you're playing entire sections of music without needing to think about every single note. Eventually, your hands "remember" what to do, and it feels natural and effortless—just like typing.

Learning a physical skill like riding a bike follows a similar pattern. At first, it feels challenging, but with practice, it becomes automatic. The first time you rode a bike, you had to use all of your focus to balance, pedal, and hold on to the handlebars. Your brain created new neural pathways for riding a bike for the first time. And the more you practiced, the easier it got, and the less you had to concentrate. Now you can ride on autopilot because those neural pathways are strong. These pathways are activated the moment you sit on the bike, allowing you to let your mind drift or to ride without much concentration.

Take a look at Destin, who was experimenting with his bicycle to test this concept of learned neural pathways. You may know that when you turn your handlebars to the right, you steer the bike to the right. And when you turn your handlebars to the left, the bike steers left. Destin disassembled his bike and reversed this mechanism, making it steer in the opposite direction that he turned the handlebars. At first, it was incredibly challenging for him to ride the bike, but after some time, he learned how to ride it topsy-turvy. Destin continued this reverse biking method long enough for this method (and its neural pathways) to embed in his brain. After a few months, he reassembled the bike to its proper steering setting to explore this phenomenon further. And to his astonishment, although he had ridden a regular bike for decades before this experiment, he could no longer ride it since the neural pathways for this reverse method had become engrained. You can actually watch this play out in action; go to the YouTube channel *Smarter Every Day*, and search for "The Backwards Brain Bicycle."

The more you practice information, the stronger a pathway will become. Practice makes perfect. The same way you can learn to ride a bike on autopilot, your brain can learn to experience pain automatically. To unlearn pain, you must stop activating the old neural pathways and start building new ones. Unlearning pain, or any other neural pathway, is like paving a new path in an overgrown forest. By walking through the wild grass and branches over and over, you push the overgrowth aside and trample down the weeds, forming a smooth, paved path that becomes easy to walk on or even run through.

Being in pain can feel lonely and scary, but it's important to know that you are not alone. Actually, one in five people have chronic pain, just like you! And as you now understand, your pain is real, no matter what. All pain comes from the brain, even if there isn't a physical reason for it. Even when your pain is a mistake, your brain activates a neural pathway to create it.

Instead of going down the same old path that continues to create the same pain, let's agree to pave a new path together. Instead of responding to your pain with fear, frustration, and dread, which only reinforces the pathways, let's embark on a new journey.

JOURNALING ABOUT PAIN

Journaling is a practical way to keep track of your symptoms and triggers so you can recognize patterns that lead to increases in pain. It also helps increase self-awareness of your fears so they are easier to bear. This awareness can help you pause and decrease the intense energy that accompanies your pain triggers, making you more capable of approaching them calmly and rationally.

Before you try journaling on your own, take a look at the stories and journal entries of two teens who, just like you, are struggling with pain.

TAYLOR'S STORY: IF ONLY THE PAIN WOULD DISAPPEAR

Taylor is a fifteen-year-old student who dreams of attending medical school and becoming a surgeon. She has been experiencing recurring migraines since she started at an intense college preparatory high school. Because of her constant symptoms, she struggles with studying and test performance. She has gone to multiple doctors, and none have found any specific underlying cause for her migraines. Some told her she just had anxiety, and others prescribed medications to manage the pain. Taylor worries that her symptoms will never go away and stresses that the pain might prevent her from achieving the grades she needs to get into the "right" colleges and reach her goal of becoming a surgeon.

TAYLOR'S JOURNAL ENTRY. I am not afraid of my pain, but I am worried that whatever is causing the pain will prevent me from doing the things I want to do, like hanging out with my friends, playing sports, and studying. The schools I need to get into are so competitive. I'm up against people who get almost perfect grades, so studying less is really not an option for me. Though my pain is intense, I think I prefer it to the nausea or light sensitivity that sometimes comes along with my migraines. I can push through the pain. It's way harder to read and study when the auras come. If the pain and accompanying nausea and light sensitivity would disappear, I imagine that I could sit and study without having to constantly take breaks, turn the lights off, or close my eyes. I imagine waking up with a clear head, confident and calm. I could open up my bedroom curtains without fear that it would trigger a headache. I could get on the bus, sit through class, do my homework, and complete my final exams without constantly needing to push through pain. Although I can do what I have to at home and at school, none of it is easy. I fantasize about a life where I can do all that without struggling through pain. My goal is to have fewer migraines per week. The thing that will stand in my way is wanting to identify the root cause of my pain, and feeling like the harder I try to find a reason, the more intense my migraines get.

JUAN'S STORY: GETTING BACK TO THE BASEBALL FIELD

Sixteen-year-old Juan is a talented baseball player. About one year ago, he was injured while playing in a championship baseball game. Although his doctor informed him that his injury healed beautifully, he still experiences pain anytime he plays sports, walks for an extended time, or does strenuous activities. His pain was so intense that he stopped playing baseball and started spending more time at home. Juan's grandmother has been attentive and understanding, allowing him to sit on the couch and play video games more often.

JUAN'S JOURNAL ENTRY. It's been over a year since my injury, and all the doctors say it healed months ago, but the pain is still here. I've had several MRIs and scans, and though the doctors say everything is fine now, it doesn't feel fine. I keep thinking they must be missing something.

I'm so sick and tired of being in pain. But even though I miss playing baseball and hanging out with my friends, it feels nice to have less pressure and be at home right now. I have a huge family, and staying home while everyone is out during the day means I get some quiet. Plus, Abuela's always around. Since I got hurt, Abuela's been spoiling me more than anyone else—making my favorite foods, constantly checking on me, and being a lot less strict about letting me watch TV and play video games.

I want to feel better and return to playing sports and hanging out with my friends. If the pain disappears, I'll stop missing out on things that I enjoy. I miss the excitement and pride I felt when playing sports, especially baseball. I imagine scoring the winning home run and the whole school cheering me on—I feel unstoppable. But I don't know if I am that good anymore—I haven't played for so long. I'm scared of getting back to the baseball field and disappointing everyone. I think that might be the biggest thing standing in my way—leaving all the safe, calm stuff I enjoy at home only to disappoint everyone. What if I try, and everyone expects me to return to how I was before? Will Abuela stop giving me so much attention? Will she stop letting me play video games? Although I want to get better, the thought of losing the things I've gotten used to scares me.

Fantasize what your life might look like without pain. Describe what you see in your fantasy. How will it look different from now? It might help to first describe what a typical day looks like now, and then how it would look in your fantasy. You might want to describe what you will be doing that you aren't able to do now.

On the lines that follow, write your journal entry. If you need more space, no worries—grab another sheet of paper!

In this chapter, you learned about how the brain takes in sensory information and sends distress signals to the body in the form of pain. You fantasized a new paved path to lead you to complete recovery. You learned:

- That the brain has the final say and signals pain when it perceives a threat to the body
- How neurons, the brain's messengers, form neural pathways that facilitate learning
- That the more you practice a behavior or action, the stronger those neural pathways become
- That you can learn pain by forming and strengthening neural pathways and unlearn pain by creating new pathways

FINDING EVIDENCE AND EMBRACING A NEW PATH

You just finished learning about how your brain processes incoming sensory information, creating neural pathways to enable quick and smooth responses. You also now understand that your brain decides what body signals to make, like how much pain to signal, based on how much danger it predicts. But how can you evaluate how much danger you are really in?

This chapter will transform you into a detective, searching for clues and evidence that inform you whether your pain is due to physical damage or your brain's faulty learning. With PRT, the first goal is to speak to your cognitive brain—the part of you that understandably believes there is something wrong with your body. After all, when you feel pain, your brain is wired to attribute it to physical damage. For example, if your elbow hurts after playing handball with classmates, your brain might think, *I must have hurt my elbow playing handball.* If your stomach hurts after lunch, your brain might think, *That food hurt my stomach.* If your throat hurts after choir, your brain might think, *All that singing hurt my throat.* In these situations, your brain is trying to help you. It wants to keep you out of harm's way—you get the idea! Your job is to find the cause for the body signal: Is there a real danger, or is this pain just a false alarm?

In chapter 1, you peeked behind the curtain when responding to questions about your pain. You then reviewed explanations about why those questions are relevant and how your answers can help decipher whether your pain is neuroplastic or from an injury. But let's unpack this further so that your cognitive brain understands how to apply this skill to your chronic pain.

You'll learn about two patients with chronic pain and see if you can solve their pain mystery using the neuroplastic pain criteria. Let's take a fresh look at these criteria:

- Symptoms began with no injury or long after an injury occurred.
- Pain persists after the normal course of healing.
- Symptoms started during a stressful time.
- Symptoms are inconsistent, move, vary, or behave in a way that normal acute pain does not.
- Doctors are unable to explain what's going on.
- You have or have had multiple symptoms.
- You have symmetrical symptoms (for example, both arms, both legs, or both wrists).
- Triggers unrelated to your body bring on pain (for example, weather, location, or time of day).
- Symptoms increase with stress and decrease with calm.
- You put a lot of pressure on yourself, are self-critical or perfectionistic, or tend to engage in people pleasing.
- You have anxiety, depression, or other mental health conditions.
- You have family members with chronic pain, anxiety, depression, or other mental health conditions.

As you read about Elijah's pain experience, look for clues pointing to a neuroplastic pain diagnosis.

ELIJAH'S PAIN: SEARCHING FOR EVIDENCE

Elijah is sixteen years old and has had lower back pain for three years. His pain first began while he was moving to a new state with his mother. Although he was upset about leaving all of his friends, Elijah realized he didn't have much choice, so he made the best of it. On the day of the move, Elijah carried many heavy boxes and furniture into a moving truck, and later helped unpack everything when they arrived. It makes sense to Elijah that his back hurt after this strenuous activity since he did a lot of heavy lifting. But the pain never went away. After a few months, Elijah went to his doctor for a back scan, but the doctor saw nothing abnormal on his X-ray. Yet Elijah feels pain every time he sits down, but he can lie flat, stand, and walk without any pain. His pain is strongest while sitting in class, particularly while taking exams.

Elijah loves to watch football—he is a fanatic. He never misses a game, knows all the players' stats, and owns more team merch than he knows what to do with. This past year, his home team, the Detroit Lions, made the playoffs. He couldn't contain his excitement. The Lions would play in the Super Bowl with just a couple more wins. He couldn't wait to host a watch party! Elijah was ready: Drinks and snacks lined the table, his two best friends sat on his couch with him, and he wore his lucky jersey.

Elijah began watching the game as always, pacing around the room, partly to ease his nervous energy, and also because he avoids sitting at all costs. The game began, and the Lions were on fire from the first kickoff. When they scored a touchdown, Elijah cheered and went to the couch to high-five his friends. He watched intently, not taking his eyes off the TV for a second. After a few minutes, the team scored another touchdown—cheers all around! During the next commercial break, Elijah and his friends broke down the play strategies, going over each player's moves. Only then did Elijah realize that he had been sitting for the last forty minutes without any back pain. Elijah couldn't remember any instance of sitting without pain in the previous couple of years. The pain immediately returned, and he still can't figure out why and how that happened.

Below is a sample evidence list we created with Elijah to help him gather clues indicating neuroplastic pain.

EVIDENCE LIST

Physical injury	Neuroplastic problem
Lifting boxes	pain began during stress
Moving furniture	pain began with no injury
Hurts when he sits	Doctor couldn't find a physical explanation
	Pain persisted long after the normal course of healing
	Pain is not present when lying, standing, walking
	Pain suddenly disappeared when doing something enjoyable
	Pain immediately returned when he thought about it
	Pain is strongest while sitting in class, taking exams

Elijah's story is an excellent example of how gathering evidence can help you clarify a neuroplastic diagnosis. He has so much evidence to help his cognitive brain begin to understand that he might not have a physical problem. The most compelling evidence is that if Elijah can sit without pain even once, it proves that the physical position of sitting is not what is triggering his pain. If something in Elijah's spine were compressed or aggravated from sitting, he would have pain every time he sat in that same position. There would be no exceptions. Therefore, there must be something else at play when it comes to his pain—his brain.

Let's break this down. Elijah's brain learned to associate sitting with pain. As you know, the brain's primary role is protecting you from harm. The brain has many different ways of accomplishing this. It can go to great lengths to keep you safe and learn to anticipate threats by creating associations. These associations result in conditioned responses. A conditioned response is a learned reaction that often prevents you from repeating dangerous behaviors.

CONDITIONED RESPONSES AND LEARNED ASSOCIATIONS

Ivan Pavlov, a famous Russian scientist, helped us understand how the phenomenon of conditioned responses works. Pavlov noticed that the dogs in his lab would salivate when they received food. He then rang a bell before bringing their food and noticed that, over time, the dogs started to salivate to the sound of the bell even without food (Pavlov 1927).

Pavlov called the food an unconditioned stimulus and the dogs' salivation an unconditioned response because a dog's brain doesn't need to learn the association between food and salivation—the salivation response is automatic. He called the bell a neutral stimulus because, unlike food, a dog's brain does not naturally associate a bell's ring with eating. Pavlov's experiment showed that your brain can learn to associate a neutral stimulus with any outcome through learning and repetition.

Thousands of years ago, when humans had to gather their food in the wild, they might have picked fruits and berries. If they ate poisonous berries and got sick, their brains might have associated those berries with nausea to prevent them from eating them again. This conditioned response, or association, is an adaptive protective mechanism, meaning that it is a beneficial way the brain learns to keep you safe.

But you also know that the brain can sometimes make mistakes and continually make the same mistake if the neural pathways for that error are strong. For example, what if your ancestors were to get nauseous from all kinds of berries? What if every safe strawberry and blueberry were to trigger nausea because of the association their brains created? You might recognize this response if you ever ate a specific food while you were sick with a virus. If the virus led to nausea and vomiting, your brain might associate the food with nausea even though the food had nothing to do with your vomiting. Your brain may create an association and response of nausea to that food for a long time. Even the mere sight of that particular food might trigger nausea due to conditioned learning.

You may have already caught on to how this fits in with the example you read about Elijah. Elijah learned to associate sitting with pain. It was not necessarily the sitting causing the pain, but rather his interpretation of sitting as a threatening activity. Pain can become linked with safe physical positions, activities, and more. Just because both the sun rises and the rooster crows in the morning does not mean the rooster makes the sun rise. Just because you experience pain during or after a specific activity does not mean that activity causes the pain. The pain comes from your mind's interpretation of the activity as threatening, not the activity itself.

Let's dive into one more story, this time about a girl named Kim. As you read about Kim's pain, gather and write down any evidence that suggests neuroplastic and physical causes of her pain.

KIM'S PAIN: SEARCHING FOR EVIDENCE

Kim is fourteen years old and started high school this year. She has been experiencing severe stomach aches, bloating, diarrhea, and occasional headaches since September, and it is already spring! Kim's foster mom has taken her to many doctors about her persistent pain symptoms. Doctors and scans have found no signs of tissue damage but say that the symptoms she reports are consistent with a diagnosis of irritable bowel syndrome. Her primary doctor explained that there is little to do except manage her symptoms with medication, eat a fiber-filled diet, and see a therapist to manage her anxiety. Although Kim has experienced anxiety, she doesn't think it explains her bloating and diarrhea.

Kim was on the tennis and soccer teams at her middle school, but avoided trying out for sports at the start of the year. She was afraid that the pain would start while she was playing or that she would need too many bathroom breaks. Now, she doesn't even want to go to school because she is afraid that she will be in pain during class and need the bathroom, and that her new friends will judge her. Her stomach feels a lot better when she is at home with her foster mom and intensifies when her foster mom leaves the house without telling her and when she anticipates change.

Now try to fill in as many clues as you can find to complete Kim's evidence list:

EVIDENCE LIST

Physical injury	Neuroplastic problem

Kim's story is another representation of what so many people with chronic pain experience. Like Elijah, Kim has a lot of compelling evidence but might find it challenging to accept that her pain has a neuroplastic component because she received a diagnosis from her doctor. When a doctor tells you something is wrong, you will likely trust them because they are the experts. You may feel relieved to receive a diagnosis, even if that might mean something is wrong with your body. Sometimes, the uncertainty of not knowing what is wrong feels even worse than hearing that something is wrong. Well-meaning doctors are trained to look for and rule out physical problems, not brain-wiring problems.

IS YOUR PAIN A HARDWARE OR A SOFTWARE PROBLEM?

A good way to understand this concept is to think about your body as being like a computer or phone. The hardware consists of the physical components: the screen, buttons, speaker, and camera. If your phone falls on the floor and the screen cracks, you have a hardware problem to fix. Similarly, if you fall and break your ankle, you have a physical problem and must go to the doctor to fix it. Now consider the software of your computer or phone, which consists of the programs, apps, storage, and the cloud. If there is a glitch or a bug with your iPhone's system, you need tech support to fix your software problem. Similarly, when you have neuroplastic pain, you have a software problem and need to target your brain instead of your body. Your brain's "software" is glitching, responding to your "hardware" as if it were broken when it is perfectly intact.

Some diagnoses describe a cluster of symptoms rather than identifying the root problem. Kim's irritable bowel syndrome diagnosis does just that: Her GI tract is contracting and causing irritability, and she experiences many of the same symptoms as other people who receive that diagnosis. The diagnosis is a description of those symptoms, not their cause. In another example, fibromyalgia is characterized by unexplained, widespread body pain. Again, this diagnosis does not identify the symptoms' cause, but describes them. Using a medical diagnosis to label symptoms reinforces that a hardware problem is present and needs a physically targeted intervention. But if you have neuroplastic pain, you have a software problem, and the correct treatment is a mind-body intervention. Just like you can fix software glitches, you can retrain your brain to stop sending unnecessary pain signals.

YOUR PAIN: SEARCHING FOR EVIDENCE

Now that you have become a neuroplastic pain detective and uncovered clues about Elijah's and Kim's pain, try to start an evidence list for your own symptoms.

As you immerse yourself in this detective work, you will become the expert on your body and pain. **When you find clues or evidence, jot them down on this evidence list.**

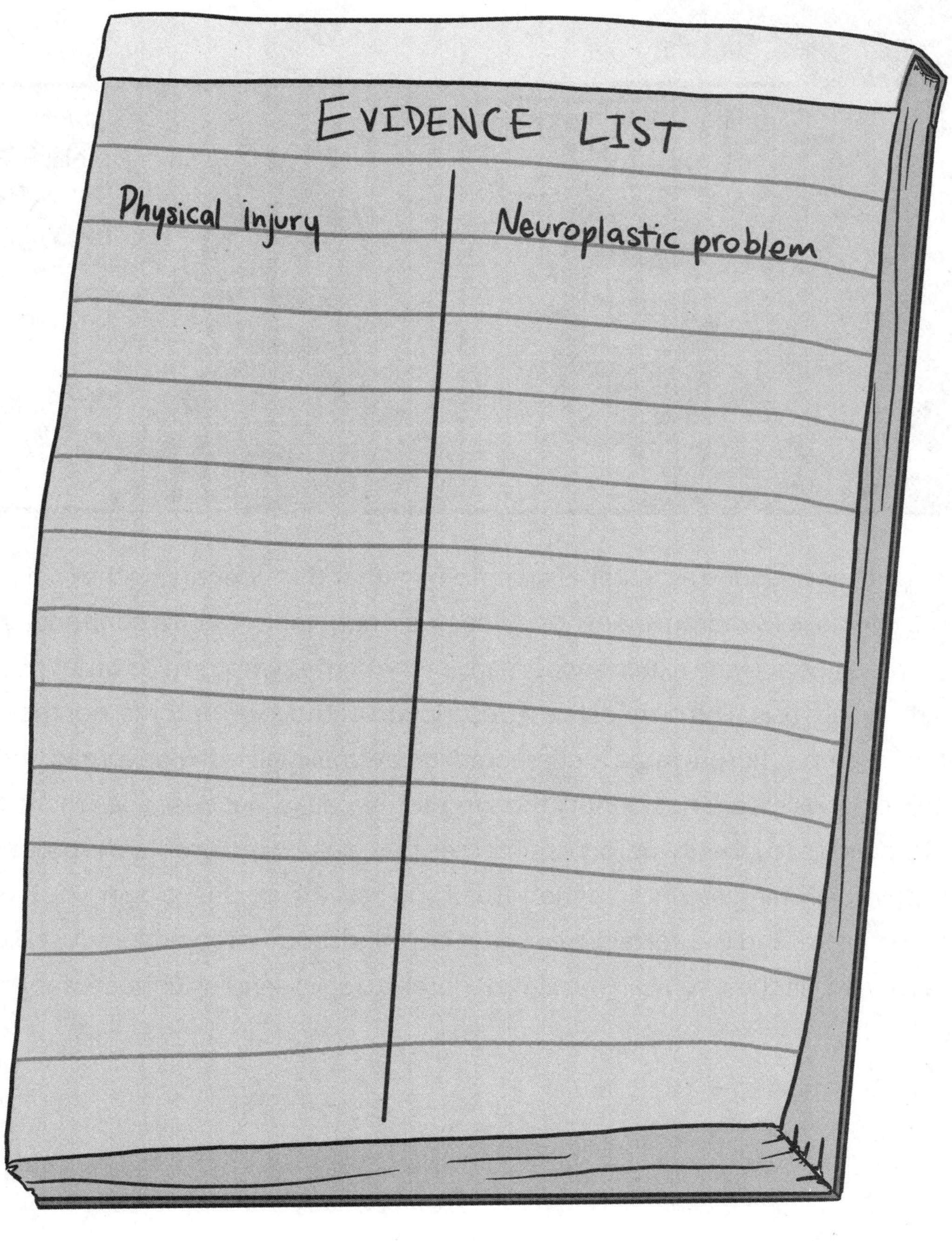

You will start to understand how your pain behaves and become more aware of what makes it better and what makes it worse. As you know, the brain creates pain when it believes you are in physical danger. But when you authentically know your body is safe, your brain will get the message and deactivate pain signals. So, gathering and reinforcing evidence plays a significant role in getting your cognitive brain on board and will soon lead you to the next step: turning off your pain.

It can be challenging to believe that your pain is entirely neuroplastic. You've probably been receiving the opposite message ever since your pain started, or you received a medical diagnosis like Kim's. You are evolutionarily hardwired to associate physical pain with physical damage. Like Elijah, you may have unconsciously learned associations that create pain in response to neutral, nondangerous situations. For all these reasons, it makes complete sense that you were trying to apply physical or medical treatments to your pain. We would have done the same thing! But when you continuously search for a physical problem, you reinforce the idea that there is something physical to fix. And there's nothing more threatening to your nervous system than believing an ongoing threat exists, especially when it doesn't!

Receiving diagnoses might have felt hopeful—like you've finally found an answer to this unrelenting pain. But when treatments end in disappointment, it's understandable that you'd be more hesitant the next time. This workbook helps address precisely what the medical treatments missed.

This chapter mainly addressed your cognitive brain to help you reach a neuroplastic determination. In the next chapter, you will see that your pain is neuroplastic and gain evidence through the implementation of PRT tools.

In this chapter, you learned to search for clues and evidence to help determine whether your pain is due to physical damage or your brain's faulty learning. You explored:

- Common criteria pointing to a neuroplastic diagnosis
- Gathering evidence
- Challenges to accepting a neuroplastic diagnosis, including biology, conditioned responses, and medical diagnoses

CALMING YOUR PRIMITIVE BRAIN: TOOLS TO RECOVER

Up to this point, you have learned why you experience pain and how chronic neuroplastic pain develops. You even gathered your own evidence that your pain is likely neuroplastic. So now what? How do you get rid of your unnecessary pain?

YOUR DOWNSTAIRS BRAIN

Your cognitive brain is responsible for figuring things out and thinking things through. So far, your cognitive brain guided you through the first four chapters of this workbook and helped you understand how and why you learn and reinforce neural pathways. Now, let's focus on another part of your brain called your primitive, or instinctual, brain, sometimes known as your "downstairs" brain. This part of your brain is like an emergency system that responds automatically to threats without much thought or planning. It is the first part of the brain to form and is already well developed in infancy. It is located at the very base of the brain and includes your brain stem, limbic system, and amygdala.

These brain areas involve reflexes, instincts, and emotions. The amygdala is the part of your brain responsible for the automatic responses and impulses that aim to protect you in anticipation of threats. When it senses a threat, your cognitive brain typically goes offline, leaving you with only your instincts, which act faster and more effectively when in danger.

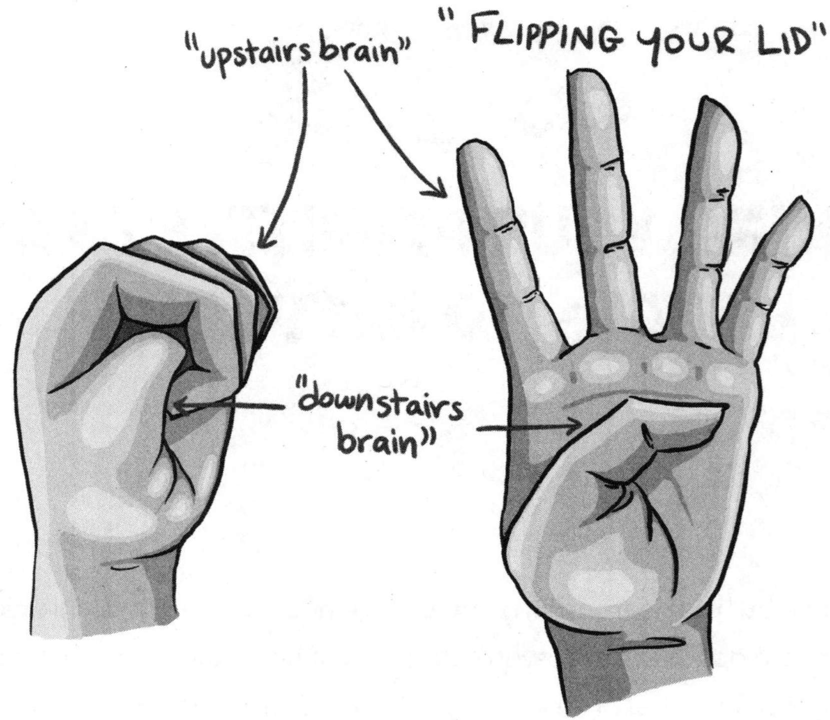

To help you understand this concept, take a look at how psychiatrist Dan Siegel explains the way different parts of the brain work together, specifically when you feel threatened or unsafe (Siegel 2010). Take this hand model of the brain:

Imagine your brain is like your hand. Try this: make a fist, tucking your thumb beneath your other fingers. Your other fingers represent your cognitive or upstairs brain, which consists of your prefrontal cortex, the thinking and planning part of your brain that is in charge of complex functions like planning, judgment, and self-control. Your thumb represents your primitive or downstairs brain, responsible for your survival instincts, emotions, and automatic reactions like fight or flight. Now, quickly open your hand. When you perceive a threat in your environment, you are metaphorically flipping your lid, leaving your thumb exposed and requiring it to work alone. This analogy represents your upstairs brain going offline as you shift into survival mode. Your primitive brain takes over, making you more likely to misinterpret reality and react impulsively based on emotion and fear rather than reason.

When you experience fear or pain, you can easily flip your lid, switching your cognitive brain off and leaving your primitive brain in charge. Although you can tell your cognitive brain it is safe, the instinctual brain does not engage in reasoning. Therefore, you have to show your instinctual brain that it is safe so that it feels safe.

Imagine you come home one day, stroll into your bathroom, and see a big shadow behind your shower curtain. Your first thought might be, *There's a stranger in my shower!* You can run into another room, lock the door, and tell yourself repeatedly that you are safe and that there is no way that shadow is a person. But as much as you tell yourself that, you will still feel scared. But, if you can muster up the courage to open the bathroom door and pull back the shower curtain, you will reveal all your familiar belongings: your shampoos, loofa, bath bombs, and washcloth. When you've confronted the unknown and confirmed that there is no danger, your fear can dissipate, allowing you to feel safe.

It takes a lot of courage to peek behind the curtain. It might feel easier to avoid opening it altogether. But for the fear to subside, you must confront what you are scared of. In the same way, to overcome your fear of your pain, you are going to have to face it. It might feel scary at first, but eventually, the fear will dissipate once you see the pain for what it is—sensations, expectations, memories, and conditioning.

SOMATIC TRACKING

Somatic tracking is a PRT tool that can help you peek behind the curtain and show your instinctual brain that it is safe. It retrains your brain and threat detection system to interpret incoming information correctly. It allows you to approach your pain and see that there is no threat. In this way, you start to respond differently and eliminate fear so the pain loses its fuel, and you experience only a neutral sensation. If this sounds a bit abstract, don't worry—it will become more clear as you begin practicing this somatic exercise.

pain = sensation + fear

~~pain~~ = sensation + ~~fear~~

Before we practice somatic tracking, let's set the stage to prepare you for success. First, observe your current responses to pain. What is your initial thought when your pain first comes on? **You can circle any that apply to you or fill in your own on the blank line.**

Uh oh, the pain is going to get much worse.

My pain will never go away.

My day is ruined.

Why is the pain here—did I do something wrong?

How did I hurt myself?

Why does this only happen to me?

Fill in your own automatic thought: ______________________________

Do these thoughts make you feel more stressed and scared? Or do they make you feel safe and reassured? Often, our automatic thoughts are inaccurate, producing unnecessary fear. As you know, when your brain perceives danger, it will likely react with more pain!

Instead, let's interrupt the fear thought and replace it with a more accurate message that also communicates safety to your brain.

HOW TO COMMUNICATE SAFETY

To help you confront your pain, let's find some things you can say to yourself to help you feel brave and empowered. When you feel empowered, you are likely more prepared to do something difficult. Now that you understand how pain works and that your neuroplastic symptoms are mainly a false alarm, you can come up with safety messages that feel authentic to you based on the evidence you have gathered. Here is a list of safety messages that have helped others prepare for the next activity:

My body is strong.

This pain is temporary.

My pain isn't always like this.

I've felt this before, and I was okay.

I am safe.

There is nothing that I need to do to protect my body.

I am not going to injure myself by moving.

There is nothing wrong with my body.

I am capable of recovering.

Pain doesn't mean something terrible is happening.

Write down some safety messages that feel right to you:

Now let's practice tuning in to your inner calm to prepare, ground, and support you before you move into somatic tracking, which might feel unfamiliar. When you feel anxious, you may feel out of control and lose sight of your inner calm. You have a natural state of peacefulness that is always present, though stressors can disrupt it and grab your attention. Let's take a moment to become mindful of your inner state of calm.

ACTIVITY ACCESS YOUR INNER CALM

Color this lake with soft pastel colors that bring you a sense of calm and peace.

Drawing is thought to relax the amygdala by deactivating the fight-flight response. Research shows that coloring and drawing decreases anxiety by taking your mind's focus away from your fears and produces a calming effect (Bosomtwe et al. 2022; Brechet, D'Audigier, and Audras-Torrent 2020; Burton and Baxter 2019; Drake 2021; Drake and Winner 2013). But what does calm feel like in your body? Let's find out!

ACTIVITY BODY AWARENESS BREATHING

To listen to an audio recording of this exercise, visit **http://www.newharbinger.com/56838**.

Sit back comfortably in your chair, and give yourself a moment to breathe in through your nose. As you inhale, simply notice the sensation of your breath. Notice the stream of air tickling your nostrils. It may feel cool or smooth. Observe your chest expand with your inhale, and allow your gaze to follow that breath down to your stomach. Let your stomach fill and inflate with air like a balloon. Then, slowly exhale and feel your stomach empty and deflate. Observe the feeling of your breath as it returns through your chest and escapes from your mouth. You might notice your breath stream feels warmer on its way out of your mouth when you exhale. As you continue to breathe in deeply and out slowly and softly, notice your natural breathing pace. Allow your breath to go at whatever pace feels natural and comfortable.

If you find it challenging to find your inner calm, don't worry; that's normal when you first begin using this exercise. Below are some tips to help guide you:

- Try a pace of a slow count of 4 for the in-breath and a slow count of 7 for the out-breath.
- You can also try a slow count of 4 for the in-breath, holding your breath for another count of 4, and then a slow count of 7 for the out-breath.
- Place one hand on your stomach and one on your chest, and take in a deep breath. Which hand elevates higher? If your stomach rises more than your chest, you're doing it correctly! You want to make sure you're breathing all the way into your belly, and not stopping short at your chest.

Great job! You just practiced your first mindfulness exercise. Mindfulness is the simple practice of observing without judgment. Paying attention to the sensation and pace of your breath with mindfulness can help you relax. But why? Your body has a built-in nervous system that regulates your stress levels. You have your sympathetic nervous system, the "gas pedal" that pushes you to react to stress, and your parasympathetic nervous system, which acts as a "brake pedal," returning your body to calm. Deep breathing activates your parasympathetic nervous system and allows you to rest and recover.

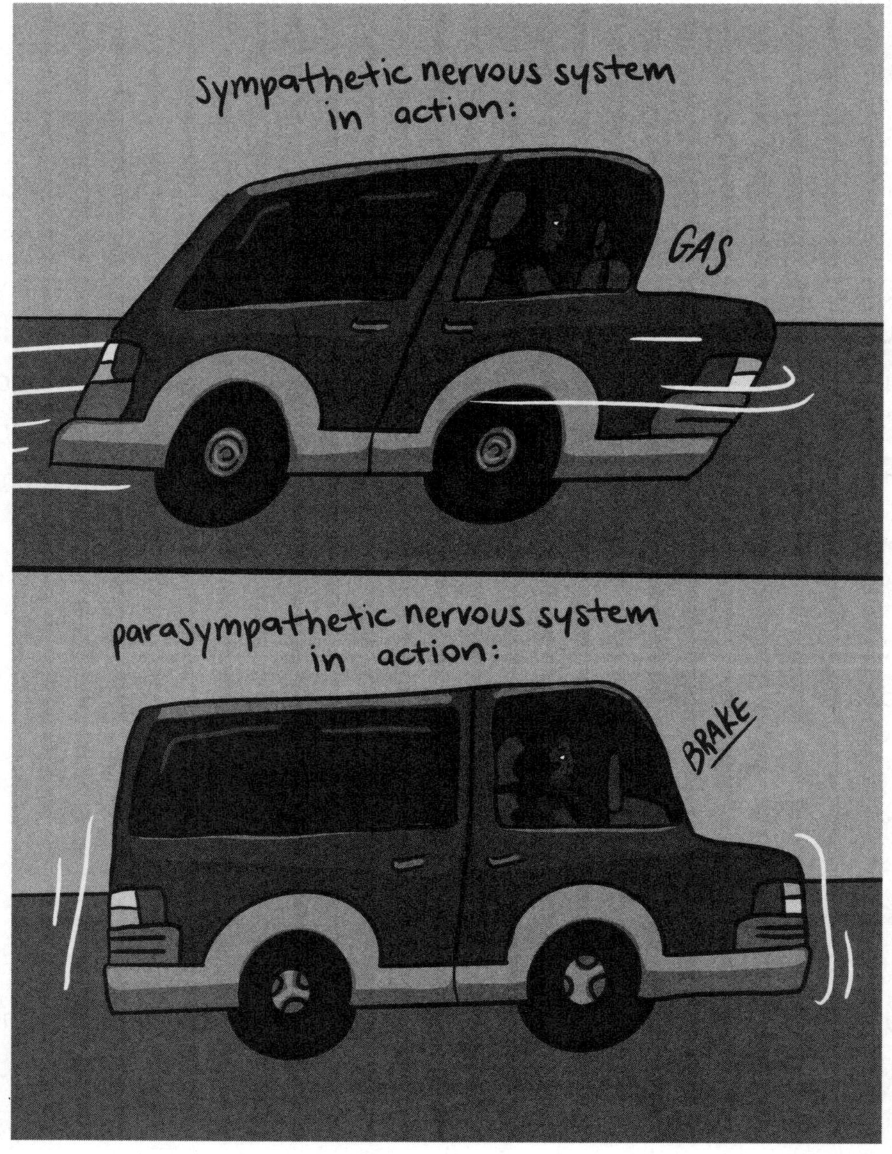

Your inner calm is always there; now you know how to access it! You can use this tool to maintain your state of calm while you tune in to your pain symptoms.

Now you are ready to try a somatic tracking exercise, and peek behind your shower curtain. Remember, to do this exercise and show your primitive brain that you're safe, you need to be experiencing some level of discomfort. You shouldn't be in intense pain, but you want to feel some discomfort so you can observe and describe it. As funny as this might sound, the pain becomes your opportunity to practice!

SOMATIC TRACKING A PEEK BEHIND THE CURTAIN

To listen to an audio recording of this exercise, visit **http://www.newharbinger.com/56838**.

Start by finding a comfortable position and taking three deep breaths, as you just practiced. When you feel like you've tapped into your inner calm, mindfully and gently shift your focus to any unpleasant sensation in your body.

Try to pay attention to the unpleasant sensation in the same nonjudgmental and gentle way you observed your breath—without pressure or intensity. There are two ways to pay attention to something. One way is to focus intensely, like when you study and memorize information for a test. But you can also focus on something with effortlessness and ease, like watching clouds pass overhead, marveling at fish in an aquarium, or observing the ocean waves at the beach. See if you can use this peaceful energy while attending to your sensations.

Now, describe the first unpleasant physical sensation you notice. We encourage you to do this aloud if you feel comfortable doing that.

Describe the location of this sensation as best as you can. Is it spread out wide or concentrated in one spot? How would you describe the quality of the sensation? Is it an ache, a tingling, a burning, or a pulsing feeling? What color or shape would the sensation be if you could see it?

Good! Remember, you are not judging the sensation or trying to make it do anything or change in any way. You are only observing with interest and curiosity. Without any judgment or specific desired outcome. You are just noticing it, getting to know it, and exploring it.

As you observe your sensations, it might feel like something is happening in your body. After all, your brain has interpreted these sensations as dangerous for so long. But you now have evidence that your body is okay. Your body is strong and adaptable and has the power to heal itself. Can you choose one statement from the safety message list you created earlier and say it out loud? Remind yourself that your brain has been overreacting to a perfectly neutral, safe sensation for a while!

What do you notice as you pay attention in this new way? Does the sensation intensify or subside? Does it move around or remain stagnant?

Whatever happens or doesn't happen is entirely okay. Allow yourself to pay attention to this sensation, knowing that you don't need to change it or get rid of it. In fact, there's nothing to get rid of!

Imagine you're watching a timelapse video of the metamorphosis of a caterpillar into a beautiful butterfly. You first notice a caterpillar crawling in the grass. Then it starts to change colors, which means it is beginning its transformation into a beautiful butterfly. You don't need to do anything to speed up or slow the process, and you don't want to stop the metamorphosis. You're just watching it happen as it will happen. You then quietly observe the caterpillar morph into a tiny greyish-brown chrysalis hanging from a bright green leaf. Within seconds, it emerges from its chrysalis, now as a beautiful, vibrant butterfly spreading its new wings. It flies through the air for the first time, lands gently on a bed of daisies, and then flies again. You don't have to chase it, you don't have to catch it, and you don't have to change its direction. You're just observing it and marveling at its graceful movements.

Focus on your sensation again and see if you can follow it like you observed the caterpillar transform into a beautiful butterfly and marveled as it fluttered through the air. Isn't it amazing that your brain can generate these sensations in different parts of your body? We bet that's different from how you usually look at these sensations. But right now, perhaps you can marvel at them and the power of your brain. Let it do what it will—it isn't dangerous. Your only task is to observe gently and communicate safety. And we know it will pass, just as it has before.

Great job!

What did you notice as you observed this sensation throughout the exercise? Did it change, intensify, subside, stay the same, or move around your body?

Whatever happens during somatic tracking is okay. The purpose of somatic tracking is to respond to pain in a new way with a new reaction: one of increased feelings of safety, mindfulness, and ease instead of fear, judgment, and frustration.

It might feel overwhelming at first—after all, you are working an entirely new muscle. Think about the first time you lifted weights or tried a new exercise. Increasing your strength is challenging until you build enough muscle to do it comfortably. It's the same way when you first use somatic tracking for pain. You are learning to respond to your pain in a completely new way, and it will be understandably challenging in the beginning. But once you get in more reps, it will become easier.

As you practice somatic tracking, you will gather important information. The pain may increase because you are paying attention to it. When this happens, you are confirming that your brain has the power to turn up the pain. If pain can intensify simply by looking at it, that is a strong piece of evidence for a neuroplastic diagnosis. In the same way, if your pain decreases, that's great evidence too. If a mindfulness exercise can change your pain in any way, it reinforces that the cause may not be tissue damage, injury, activity, or position.

The important takeaway is that decreasing pain during somatic tracking is not the goal. The goal is to change your relationship with your symptoms and reduce fear. Somatic tracking teaches you to peek behind the curtain and approach your pain with curiosity so it loses its fuel source—fear.

In this chapter, you learned that when you sense a threat, your cognitive brain goes offline and your primitive brain takes over, reacting quickly based on instinct to ensure survival. But you need to reactivate your cognitive brain to assess if there is actually a threat. You learned:

- That your primitive, instinctual, downstairs brain (brain stem, limbic system, amygdala) responds automatically, without thinking, in response to perceived threat
- That your downstairs brain's quick emotional, instinctive reactions make you more likely to misinterpret reality as dangerous since that part of your brain is not rational
- How to replace inaccurate, fear-inducing thoughts with more accurate thoughts that communicate safety to your brain
- To communicate safety to your brain by using breathing and mindfulness techniques
- That somatic tracking helps you respond to your pain in a new way: with feelings of safety, mindfulness, and ease instead of fear, judgment, and frustration
- How to use somatic tracking to approach your pain with curiosity and safety so that your pain loses its fuel—fear

CHOOSING YOUR PAIN-REDUCING TOOLS

In the last chapter, you practiced somatic tracking, one of the most effective PRT tools for overcoming pain-related fear. As you now know, when your fear decreases, so will your pain. It may take time, but if you trust the process and follow the steps in this workbook, you will learn to respond to your pain differently and find your way out.

Using somatic tracking for pain is like learning to swim for the first time. There are two ways to learn. The first way is to have someone throw you into the deep end. If this were to happen, you would be terrified and frantically flail around until you realized that all you had to do is stay still and you would float to the top. This method would get the job done but would be unnecessarily traumatic. The second and more preferred way would be to gradually get used to the water in a way where you feel safe. You could dip your feet in first and slowly wade in once you feel safe. When you learned to approach the water with a feeling of safety, you could learn to swim without fear.

You will use PRT techniques in the same way. You will confront the pain in a way that feels safe instead of going straight to the deep end. The techniques you use will depend on what level of pain you are in so that you gain corrective experiences. Corrective experiences happen when you expose yourself to what you fear and stay, observe, and access your inner calm. When you do this, you build new neural pathways for learning and you recognize that the sensations are not dangerous. By staying instead of avoiding, you correct your perception of that situation and reduce your fear. So, a corrective experience is not a decrease in pain but a decrease in fear.

WHEN YOUR PAIN IS HIGH: TOOLS AND TECHNIQUES

When it comes to somatic tracking, you may wonder when, how often, and for how long you should practice. Well, that depends on your pain intensity.

Rate your current pain level on this scale:

When your pain intensity is really high (7–10 on your scale), you might feel frustrated, scared, hopeless, and even self-critical. Observing the sensations with ease and curiosity at this pain level could be challenging. Doing somatic tracking when the pain is intense and your alarm system is active will only increase pain-related fear. So, what should you do when the pain intensity is high?

If you take the swimming example, the first time you get into the pool, you might wear floaties and stay close to the wall. Once you get comfortable in the shallow water, you may no longer need those floaties and might even feel less afraid. Similarly, when reducing pain-related fear, different techniques are appropriate depending on pain intensity and fear. When your pain is at a 7–10 intensity, your only job is to take care of yourself in the best way you know how. Perhaps this means watching your favorite TV show, listening to music, playing a game on your device, talking to a friend, taking a bath, practicing breathing, using ice or heating packs, or resting.

List some things that you can do to take care of yourself in this self-care menu:

YOUR SELF CARE
MENU
à la port

You'll also want to draw on your safety messages during high pain spikes. Even when the pain is intense, you can remind yourself that it is temporary and will pass, just as it has before. You can consider how this is just your brain misinterpreting signals, that your body is okay, and that unlearning pain is a process.

List some things you can say to yourself in this safety-message menu:

Engaging in self-care activities and communicating safety is exactly what you should do in moments of high pain. Taking a break to take care of yourself is not weak; it is necessary for recovery and a better and more compassionate way to teach your brain how to swim.

WHEN YOUR PAIN IS LOW TO MODERATE: TOOLS AND TECHNIQUES

You now understand when you should not use somatic tracking–but when should you practice somatic tracking? When your pain is low (1–3) to moderate (4–6) on your scale, it is a great time to wade in the water.

As you know, having a low pain level is an opportunity to practice. Without pain, you can't build new neural pathways and teach your brain that the sensations are safe. So, instead of responding to low-level pain with fear, frustration, or worry—bring it on! You know you can handle it and that this practice will only advance your healing.

It is certainly not easy to be brave in the face of something that is usually scary. But accessing your inner strength can be powerful, even if it doesn't feel entirely natural yet. You've probably heard of the saying "fake it till you make it," but did you know that there is actually science behind this?

Scientists wondered: Do you smile because you feel happy or feel happy because you smile? To investigate the relationship between facial expressions and emotions, researchers instructed people to move their faces and mouths into positions of smiles or frowns without explicitly telling them to smile or frown. When asked to rate their emotions after holding these facial positions, participants who had their faces in a smile position rated themselves as happy, and those who held their faces in frown positions rated themselves as sad, even though they weren't aware that they were smiling or frowning (Zajonc, Murphy, and Inglehart 1989).

Other studies show similar effects, proving that facial positions can affect how you feel and act. That made the scientists wonder: If altering facial expressions can change how you feel, what happens to your emotions when you change your body posture and position? Can assuming a power pose make you feel confident? It turns out that physically changing your body posture to powerful, expansive positions leads to robust feelings of power, confidence, control, and increased self-esteem (Carney, Cuddy, and Yap 2010). Making power poses actually increases feelings of empowerment! Try it for yourself!

When facing pain, see if you can empower yourself to stay with it long enough to reduce your fear and achieve a corrective experience. At first, you can try somatic tracking for just a few breath cycles—think baby steps. Perhaps you can only maintain your bravery for thirty seconds. That is entirely okay. As you build new neural pathways, you learn to associate the unpleasant sensations with safety and ease instead of fear and worry. With time, your sense of empowerment will grow, and your fear will decrease.

You may wonder how many times a day and for how long you should do somatic tracking. Although it is important to get in your reps, think about quality over quantity. Somatic tracking a couple of times a day when you can achieve corrective experiences is way better than pushing yourself to track every hour without regard for your pain level. How often and how long might be different for everyone. You might want to compare it to staying hydrated. Some people prefer to drink eight glasses of water at once, while others lug around a gigantic water bottle with them all day. You may like starting and ending your day with a somatic tracking exercise or prefer to practice it more frequently.

MY SOMATIC TRACKING SCHEDULE

Create your somatic tracking schedule for this week. Don't feel compelled to stick to this exact schedule. It is meant to help you figure out what keeps you *hydrated*.

Weekly Somatic Tracking Log

	Sunday	Monday	Tuesday	Wednesday	Thursday	Friday	Saturday
Time							
how many minutes?							
fear level before (1-10)							
fear level after (1-10)							

LEANING INTO POSITIVE SENSATIONS

Pain and fear can sometimes increase during somatic tracking. If that happens, you can use another tool called leaning into positive sensations. This tool is straightforward: Simply lean into (focus on and let yourself fully feel) a sensation that feels nice or pleasant. Maybe it's stopping to take a breath of fresh air, noticing the crisp change in weather or the warmth of the sun on your face, or taking a sip of tea. Perhaps it's smelling a scented candle, snuggling your pet, drawing, or gazing at a painting you love.

While living with chronic pain, your brain undoubtedly spends a lot of time noticing unpleasant feelings and less time focusing on pleasant ones. It makes sense that your brain does this—pain is much louder and can grab your attention quickly. But your brain can also get some time basking in the glory of positive sensations! Leaning into positive sensations is a tool you can use at any time by mindfully paying attention to a positive feeling or sensation. This practice helps familiarize your brain with calmness and ease instead of intensity, pain, and fear. You can also use this tool before or during a somatic tracking exercise to help settle your nerves and access your inner calm, maximizing your chance of success.

On these lines, list sensations that you find pleasant:

Let's integrate leaning into positive sensations in your somatic tracking practice. At **http://www.newharbinger.com/56838**, you'll find recordings you can download to help you practice.

TIME TO PRACTICE

As you prepare for somatic tracking, you might experience a spike of fear in anticipation of the pain. Your brain is on high alert, ready to protect you. However, you know that the pain is an inaccurate reflection of danger, so your fear is misplaced. Your goal is to actively choose to access your inner calm in the face of pain and fear.

To listen to an audio recording of this exercise, visit **http://www.newharbinger.com/56838**.

Start by taking a deep breath. Breathe fully and comfortably, slowly shifting your focus to any positive feeling you listed above—the warmth of the sun, the cool breeze on your skin, or even a nice feeling inside as you observe something beautiful outside your window. Continue breathing at an easy and comfortable pace, allowing yourself to find a sense of calm.

Good job! You are getting some practice accessing your inner calm and settling down your system. In this way, you are teaching and showing your downstairs brain that you are safe even though you are about to face your pain. Remember, you are safe even when you feel pain. Take three more nice and easy breaths. This is your home base; you can return to it any time you need.

When you are ready, shift your attention to your pain sensation. Take your time and start to explore all the things you notice about it. Where in your body is this sensation? How strong is it at this moment? Would you describe it as sharp or dull? Is there a shape to the sensation? If you could describe your pain as a color, what would it be? Can you imagine what it looks like? Is it fluctuating, moving around, pulsing in and out, or staying put?

Remember, whatever happens, your only goal is to observe and become more familiar with the sensation. You do not need to change, fix, or alter it. You are simply watching with a sense of detached curiosity and ease.

Great job! What was that like for you? Rate your pain level on a scale from 1–10, with 1 being the least painful and 10 being the most.

Good! Now that you've spent a moment with your pain sensation, shift your attention back to your chosen positive feeling. Breathe comfortably and explore that positive feeling for three more breath cycles.

Once more, switch your focus to your pain sensation. Actively attend to your pain again with interest, curiosity, or even marvel. Right now, the pain is simply an opportunity to practice. After all, your brain creates these sensations based only on its opinion. What do you notice as you attend to the sensation in this way? Has the sensation changed in any way—in quality, shape, or color? Just observe the sensation for three more breath cycles, knowing that it is only your brain's opinion and knowing that you are safe.

Great job! What was that like for you? Again, rate your pain level on a scale from 1–10, with 1 being the least painful and 10 being the most.

Before ending this exercise, take a few more mindful moments leaning into that positive feeling of choice. Let your body settle almost like you would after doing a challenging exercise. It's always important to stretch! In this way, you can literally create new neural pathways where the pain loses its fuel source and slowly becomes a simple, neutral sensation.

THE RIGHT TOOL FOR THE JOB

When framing a picture, you need to choose the right size frame. Similarly, when it comes to your pain, you want to use the right tool that fits your pain level. When the pain is intense, you may use your self-care activities, safety messaging, and leaning into positive sensations. When the pain is lower, you have an opportunity to use your somatic tracking tool, face it head-on, gain corrective experiences, and create new neural pathways!

In this chapter, you learned how to use PRT tools based on your pain intensity to gradually reduce your fear. Remember, the goal is to reduce fear which will ultimately reduce faulty pain signals! You learned:

- How to choose the right pain-reducing tool
- How to achieve a corrective experience based on your level of pain and fear
- When not to use somatic tracking
- How to use self-care and safety messages when pain intensity is high
- How to determine your frequency and duration to practice somatic tracking when pain is low/moderate
- When and how to use leaning into positive sensations
- How to access your inner calm while facing something scary (the pain)

EXPLORING EMOTIONS AND PAIN

From everything you have learned until now, you know that your beliefs and expectations have enormous power. When you believe there is a threat, or expect one, your brain is more likely to send a danger signal. As you know, pain is a danger signal, and its purpose is to warn you about threats to your physical body. You also know the brain can misinterpret danger where there is none and create pain based on faulty beliefs alone. To combat these faulty beliefs about your body and pain, you learned some tools to help you change them by targeting your cognitive brain (like using evidence lists) and your instinctual brain (like using somatic tracking). But something else that we haven't yet discussed might be fueling your pain. In this chapter, you will learn how your emotions influence your pain.

You may recall this equation from chapter 2 and the second fear umbrella from chapter 1, where you inserted other fears that might amplify your pain sensations. You see, your emotions are a big part of your brain's decision about whether to generate pain signals. This chapter will explore different emotions, the accompanying body signs, and how they might impact your pain experience.

OUR EMOTIONS PUT US IN MOTION

Emotions are mental states that involve a combination of your physiological body signs, surroundings, memories, expectations, and subsequent interpretation. It's important to remember that emotions are not inherently good or bad. Some may feel pleasant and safe, like happiness or excitement, while others may feel unpleasant and unsafe, like sadness, anger, fear, and worry. However, it's crucial to understand that all emotions are informational and motivational. They help us be efficient and productive by signaling how to respond or behave. The key is to interpret them and your situation correctly. They often come with physical signs, like a fast heartbeat, sweaty palms, shaky legs, or the sensation of butterflies in the stomach.

ACTIVITY MY BODY SIGNS

What body signs do you experience when you're feeling anxious or afraid? Place a check mark next to your anxious body signs:

☐ Racing heart	☐ Butterflies in stomach
☐ Difficulty breathing	☐ Stomach pain
☐ Dizziness	☐ Nausea
☐ Mind going blank	☐ Sweating
☐ Racing thoughts	☐ Shaky hands or legs
☐ Feeling hot or flushed	☐ Feeling like running away
	☐ Trouble falling or staying asleep

Now place a check mark next to the body signs you experience when you are feeling angry:

☐ Racing heart	☐ Tense or tight muscles
☐ Racing thoughts	☐ Stomach pain
☐ Dizziness	☐ Tightness in chest
☐ Difficulty concentrating	☐ Sweating
☐ Face turning red	☐ Feeling hot or flushed
☐ Shaky hands or legs	☐ Feeling like you want to punch something

Place a check mark next to the body signs you experience when you are feeling sad:

☐ Heaviness behind your eyes	☐ Feeling achy
☐ Lump in your throat	☐ Trouble sleeping
☐ Sleepiness	☐ Increased or decreased appetite
☐ Shortness of breath	☐ Stomach pain or constipation

The emotions themselves are not the problem. Instead, the body signs that come with your emotions can feel uncomfortable, making it difficult to think and determine whether you're in actual danger. For example, if you get nervous during an exam, your mind may go blank, making it difficult to recall the correct answers. Misinterpreting your level of danger will keep your body signs active, further impeding your ability to concentrate and access information. That level of alarm is appropriate and helpful when in actual danger but not when taking an exam or managing a social situation.

Still, emotions are important messages to pay attention to. Each emotion has a unique purpose that pushes you to take action. For example, when you feel anxious, your body alarm turns on, and the physical signs spring you into action, sending energy to your legs so you can run away fast if you are in danger. Even emotions with a bad reputation, like anger, have a purpose. For example, if you see someone bullying your friend, anger will lead you to stand up to that bully and protect your friend.

BODY SIGNS: SIGNAL OR SABOTAGE?

Sometimes, body signs can get so strong that it becomes hard to think clearly and decide how to react or what to do. Going back to the anger example, if you feel too angry, you might make the wrong decision and feel like punching the bully in the face! Soon, you'll learn how to turn down the volume of your body signs so you can think clearly and come up with an effective plan considering your situation and its consequences.

So, how do you know what emotion you are feeling? If your heart is racing, how do you know if you are scared or excited? If your chest feels heavy, how do you know if you are sad or incredibly relaxed? In other words, how does your brain decide how it will interpret your body signs?

Acting as a detective, the brain combines a few pieces of information to make sense of them. First, it senses your body signs and then collects clues from outside your body. Suppose your heart is beating very fast. In that case, your brain may search for evidence around you to figure out what's going on.

Picture this scenario: You walk into a bright and noisy room to find that all your friends are there, with smiling faces, happy birthday balloons, and tables set with colored plates and decorations. It suddenly clicks as you remember that it's almost your birthday. You've solved the mystery. You're at your surprise birthday party.

Next, your brain locates your memory of the last time you were at a surprise party. If that memory is of a pleasant and fun party, your brain expects it to be fun again. So, your brain interprets your heart racing as the emotion of excitement. However, if you didn't know who to sit with the last time you were at a party or couldn't think of what to say to your friends, you might expect the situation to feel uncomfortable. Your brain then might interpret your racing heart as anxiety.

In other words, when your brain notices your physical body signs, it combines them with your present situation and memories of past experiences to create a label or interpretation. To simplify it, the equation below will help you solve the next case.

TIRED

HOPELESS

Bored

LOVING

calm

BRAVE

JEALOUS

ANXIOUS

EXCITED

Remember, your brain makes these calculations incredibly fast. You might be unaware that your brain is calculating these equations and identifying your emotions in less than a second!

Imagine you feel your heart racing (body sign). You look around and notice that you're at your dentist's office (situation). In this case, your brain might locate your memory of getting a shot or a filling the last time you were at the dentist, so your brain expects this visit to be painful again (memory). So, what is your emotion label? If you labeled your heart racing as the emotion of fear or anxiety, you have cracked the case!

Now, you will get the chance to practice on your own.

LABELING AND TRACKING EMOTIONS

Each example describes a body sign and a different situation. **Choose an emotion label for each. We've chosen the first one for you.**

BODY SIGN	SITUATION	MEMORY/WHAT I EXPECT	EMOTION
HEART RACING	I'm at my dentist's office.	Last time, I got a filling. So I expect it will be bad again!	ANXIETY
HEART RACING	I'm in my Hip-Hop class.	Last time, I liked the class even though it was hard. So I expect I will have fun today!	
DIZZY HEAD	It's the end of gym class, and I forgot to bring water.	Last time I forgot water, I got dizzy. So I expect the dizziness is from lack of water.	
DIZZY HEAD	I'm taking a really hard math test, and I don't think I'm prepared.	Last time I took a math test, I got dizzy and forgot the answers. So I expet to forget and fail this test.	

As you can see, your brain assigns a different emotion label to your body sign depending on what is happening around you, your memories, and your expectations.

This week, keep track of any time you feel an emotion. When you notice an emotion, pay attention to what was happening at the time or right before, what you were thinking or expecting, and which body signs you sensed.

DATE & TIME	SITUATION (WHERE WAS I, WHAT JUST HAPPENED, WHAT WAS I DOING?)	MY BODY SIGNS (HEART RACING, HOT, BUTTERFLIES, SHAKY HANDS AND FEET...)	MY THOUGHT (WHAT I WAS THINKING OR EXPECTING IN THIS SITUATION)	LABEL MY EMOTION (SAD, ANGRY, WORRIED, HAPPY, EXCITED, JEALOUS, FRUSTRATED, WEAK...)

AVOIDANCE AND POWERLESSNESS

When we feel unsafe, we often try to make ourselves feel better by avoiding what is making us feel unsafe. Avoidance might make you feel like you're okay in the short term. As soon as you avoid the feared situation, your body signs of anxiety subside, and you literally feel better. But this seemingly positive result leads to the false belief that avoidance always keeps you safe. When you are safe, avoidance will increase fear and might even make you feel powerless in the long run. It reinforces the beliefs "I cannot handle this situation" and "The only way for me to be safe is to escape." This response will unintentionally confirm to your brain that you're in danger when, in fact, you are not.

Let's see how this can play out in real life. Imagine you missed a bunch of school days because of your pain. Returning to missed lessons, a stack of homework assignments, and sports tryouts might feel overwhelming! When you feel overwhelmed or anxious, you may experience uncomfortable physical sensations that you want to run from. To feel better in the short term, you may stay in the comfort of your home and avoid returning to school. However, the longer you avoid your school and friends, the bigger your anxiety and sense of powerlessness grows. Avoiding prevents you from staying for long enough to reinterpret school as safe. Instead, use the opportunity to see that you can cope and figure out what to do. When you face your fear, you teach your brain that you are capable of managing your anxiety and readjusting.

Doing this may sound a bit scary—but remember, just like with the pain, you are going to take baby steps. We are not going to throw you into the deep end. Instead, you will learn to regulate your emotions and return gradually.

WHAT DO EMOTIONS HAVE TO DO WITH IT?

You might wonder why you are reading about emotions in a workbook about eliminating pain. Before going further, let's answer the question "How do your emotions impact your pain?" Well, you've learned that when your brain thinks you're in danger, it turns on your body's alarm system, producing body signs that launch you into action. One of the body signs the brain creates is pain. But your brain also creates anxiety.

In the times when cave dwellers roamed the land, we lived among animals and weren't as securely tucked away in sturdy homes. Imagine that a time machine transports you to those ancient times, and you find yourself living in a tent in an open field. Before sunrise, you step outside to gather eggs from your chicken coop, milk from your cow, and berries for breakfast. And eek! You spot a lion right outside your tent opening. Your heart starts beating faster than usual, moving blood away from the parts of your body you don't need in an emergency, like your stomach and head. That may cause you to feel a racing heart, stomach pain, dizziness, shortness of breath, or your mind going blank. The heart then directs that extra blood toward the parts of your body that you do need, sending a lot of energy to your hands and feet so you can fight off the lion or run away. Your body's alarm system alerts you and prepares you to act so that you survive.

Now let's travel back to the present. Today, you don't usually deal with predators at every turn. Still, you may feel those same body signs in any situation that makes you anxious. Although we have evolved, our brains retain their evolutionary survival skills. Anxiety over a test can show up in your body as a stomach ache, nausea, or your brain feeling foggy. Although there is no threat of a lion jumping out at you, your brain propels you into action as if there were one.

Both pain and anxiety are danger signals that have a specific evolutionary purpose: survival. Anxiety protects you from threats in your environment, and pain protects you from threats to your body. Unsafe emotions can turn on your body's alarm system. And when your body's alarm is on, your brain will scan for signs of danger more intensely. It's almost like you are putting on danger glasses. When your danger glasses are on, you are more likely to interpret everything, including a neutral sensation, as threatening.

For example, imagine it's late, and you're watching a scary movie alone. Even if you're brave, you may jump at the sound you hear down the hall because your danger detectors are on. After watching that scary movie, your brain can't help but scan your dark, quiet house for danger, even if logically, you know there is none.

In the same way, when you are anxious about something, your brain is on high alert, scanning your environment for danger. The quietest body sign will catch your attention, causing you to perceive it as louder than it is. You might notice pain more when you're stressed or anxious, but you might not feel it as much when you're happy or doing something you enjoy. When engaged with something that makes you happy, your brain becomes more focused on your activity and positive emotions and less on scanning your environment for danger and sending pain messages to your body.

But if your brain is on high alert because it falsely expects danger, it will scan for signs of threat, keeping you in danger mode unnecessarily.

PAIN: ALARMING EMOTIONS VS. CALM EMOTIONS

Until now, we have focused on anxiety and fear, but many different emotions can impact the volume knob that turns pain intensity up or down. To simplify this idea, let's break it down into two categories: alarming emotions and calm emotions. Alarming emotions increase pain, while calm emotions decrease pain. Let's look at some of these emotions to help you spot them when they appear.

ALARMING EMOTIONS	CALM EMOTIONS
Anxious, stressed	Happy, joyful
Angry, frustrated, annoyed	Calm, relaxed
Sad, hopeless	Strong, empowered
Fearful	Safe
Lonely	Loved, connected

When you experience any alarming emotion, your brain goes on high alert. In this way, alarming emotions fuel the pain.

This concept also applies in reverse. Calm emotions extinguish the pain flames. Imagine you are laughing with your friends about a funny post you just saw on social media.

Because you are experiencing a calm emotion, the volume button is down, and you may not feel pain.

ACTIVITY EMOTION-PAIN CONNECTION

Next time you feel an emotion from the Alarming Emotion category, come back here and write down what is happening around you. **Describe the situation that is triggering your alarming emotion. What is your emotion label?**

Situation:

____

____

My emotion label:

____

Pay attention to your body signs (for example, heart racing, feeling jittery, shortness of breath, racing thoughts, lump in throat). **Describe those signs here:**

____

____

Pay attention to your level of pain. Is your pain increasing or decreasing when your body alarm is on?

____

EMOTION REGULATION: SOMATIC TRACKING AND BEYOND

You now understand the purpose of emotions, what happens to your body when you experience alarming emotions, and how your emotions impact your pain. Here's the next question: How do you turn down the volume of alarming emotions when they are unnecessary so that you can respond appropriately and reduce your pain?

You now have tools like mindfulness breathing and PRT techniques like somatic tracking, leaning into positive sensations, and safety messaging to help you change how you respond to pain. You will pull from the same toolbox to help you regulate your emotions.

Let's show you how! Once again, go to **http://www.newharbinger.com/56838** to listen to this exercise.

First, sit back comfortably and take a moment to inhale. Notice the sensation of your breath as it enters your nose. It might feel cool or even tickle as the air streams through your nostrils. As you take a deep breath, notice the feeling of your stomach expanding like a balloon. Imagine feeling so relaxed that you could float through the air, free of any cares or worries. Then, slowly exhale and notice the warm feeling of your breath leaving your mouth. Observe your natural breathing pace as you continue to breathe for another breath cycle. Allow your breath to go at whatever pace feels natural and comfortable. This breath is your home base.

Now, we want to start facing some of your more alarming emotions instead of avoiding them. But remember, we will start slowly, and you can always return to your home base. Think of a situation that makes you feel slightly anxious—something small like waking up a few minutes late or taking a pop quiz that won't impact your grade much. Imagine that situation is happening right now.

When you can visualize that slightly anxiety-inducing scenario, shift your attention inward and notice whether you feel any uncomfortable sensations in your body. Perhaps your heart starts racing, your breathing feels more constricted, or there is a lump in your throat. Whatever the sensation is, see if you can explore it with curiosity and ease. Ask yourself:

> What is the quality of the sensation? Is it a tightness, a jitter, a tingle, a constriction? Where is the sensation located? Is it in your chest, throat, stomach, or somewhere else?
>
> What would it be doing if it were to take on movement outside of your body? Would it be running, crawling, rolling, or tightening its fists and furrowing its eyebrows?
>
> If you could, what would you say to comfort it? If it's scared, what would you do to help it slow down and feel safe?

If a friend felt afraid or nervous about something and you yelled at them to stop or pushed them away, they would probably feel much worse and more scared. See if you can soothe yourself like you would soothe a close friend. Let yourself know you're okay, and maybe even give yourself a hug. Place your hand over your heart. Doing this lights up the same part of your brain as receiving a hug from someone you love. Your feelings are normal and valid. You are not alone. But you can step in and be kind to yourself now. You can care for yourself and offer a dose of compassion and self-care whenever you need it.

Continue to breathe as you lean into this sensation, and watch what happens as you attend to it in this new way. Does it spread out? Does it hold on tight and become more intense? Whatever it does is okay. Whatever happens, you are safe.

Often when anxiety comes on, we react with fear and even panic, further reinforcing to our brain that this sensation is dangerous. But if you know that this anxiety is a false alarm or an overreaction, you can take any stressful situation as an opportunity to practice regulating yourself and teaching your brain to respond in a new way.

You can do this for yourself at any time and in any place. Let's take a few more deep breaths together. Soak in that calmness and ease you can carry with you even after reading this. You can come back and use this tool whenever you need it.

In this chapter, you explored your emotions, their accompanying body signs, and how they influence your pain. You also discovered how to regulate your alarming emotions so you can think clearly and reduce unnecessary pain. You learned:

- What emotions are
- The purpose of emotions
- How we assign emotion labels based on body signs, situations, and memories
- Scary movie mode: how we can misinterpret neutral signs
- How emotions impact pain
- How to regulate alarming emotions through the use of somatic tracking

PREDICTIVE PROCESSING: EXPECTATIONS AND PAIN

You've learned why fear and other emotions contribute to the development and continuation of chronic pain. This chapter will explain how your brain makes predictions about your safety and how that impacts your pain level.

PREDICTIVE PROCESSING

The *British Medical Journal* shared a story about a construction worker who accidentally jumped from a platform and landed on a six-inch nail. The nail went straight through his boot and out the other side. He looked down at his foot, cried in intense pain, and immediately rushed to the emergency room. But surprisingly, when doctors removed his boot, they discovered that the nail had slipped right between his toes and did not even cause a scratch! His pain was genuine, but his brain had created the pain because he saw the nail pierce through his boot and panicked as he assumed that his foot was injured (Fisher, Hassan, and O'Connor 1995).

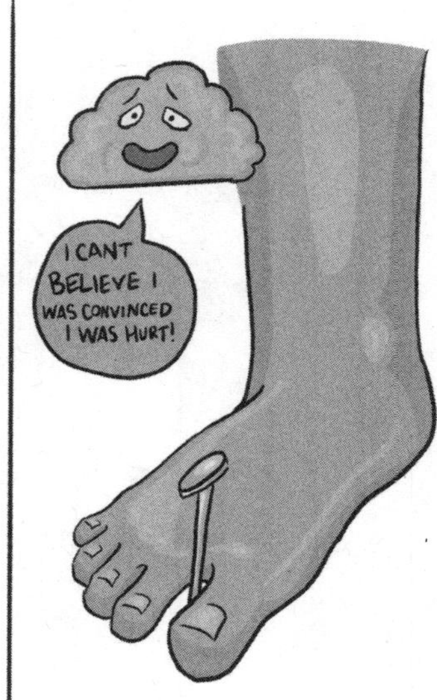

Your surroundings, beliefs, memories, and emotional state determine how much pain you feel. Some sensations may be neutral or even uncomfortable, but the intensity of the pain message will depend on how much danger your brain thinks your body is in and how quickly it wants you to react. Your brain predicts your level of safety by combining sensory information (from your sensory receptors or nerve endings) with your expectations (based on where you are, what it remembers from similar situations, and how strong your emotions and body signs are). This function is called predictive processing.

With time and experience, your brain gets better at protecting you from danger. Babies learn through trial and error, testing their environments by exploring their world through touch and play, and sometimes getting hurt in the process. Early on, they have few experiences or memories from which to predict their level of safety. As they develop, they learn and accumulate memories that help their brain assess for danger and respond accordingly. However, they also develop unnecessary fears during the process. For example, a fear of strangers can help keep kids safe. But if that fear extends to meeting new peers or teachers at school, it can become less helpful and more of an impediment.

As you get older, your ability to predict becomes faster and more automatic, often causing you to neglect considering all the information. But as your brain learns, it creates more shortcuts (by developing neural pathways, associations, and connections). Below, you will read about Ariel and his pain story. See if you can identify the role of predictive processing in the development of Ariel's pain and what unhelpful shortcuts may be contributing to the amplification of his symptoms.

ARIEL'S PAIN: PREDICTIVE PROCESSING

Ariel, the captain of his high school soccer team, injured his leg while kicking at the beginning of the season. He had to sit out for several months until his injury healed.

When he returned, he was excited but understandably hesitant to get back on the field. His team was thrilled to have him back for the most pivotal game of the season, the game that would determine whether they would make the playoffs. The last time Ariel played, he got really hurt and felt embarrassed that he couldn't finish the game. He felt he had let down his entire team. These memories began to resurface as Ariel ran down the field to get his first pass. Upon kicking the ball, he suddenly felt a sharp pain in his leg. He was in agony.

In the space below, explain why you think Ariel's brain created an intense pain signal when he kicked the ball. Include any memories or beliefs that might have contributed to his feeling pain on the soccer field.

What memories do you think Ariel's brain used to predict danger?

What expectations, beliefs, or thoughts might have magnified Ariel's pain?

As you may have guessed, Ariel's brain instantly created an intense pain signal because it expected or predicted the same injury and outcome as the last time. After his previous leg injury, his brain created a neural pathway. That pathway was activated again when receiving sensory information from his leg on the soccer field. Ariel's brain swiftly combined the physical feeling, information from his surroundings, memories from the last time he was in this situation, and his emotional response. The combination of these factors triggered the neural pathway and the pain signal. But this time, Ariel was not hurt. His pain was real, but he was not injured. Both the construction worker's and Ariel's alarm systems went off unnecessarily.

EMOTIONAL EXPERIENCE: SETTING THE STAGE FOR PAIN

You may also wonder about some of Ariel's thoughts, fears, and beliefs that set the stage for his amplified pain. Soccer means a lot to him and his identity. He is the captain of his team; the other players rely on him, and he is afraid of disappointing them, his coach, his family, and the fans in the stands. His teammates' excitement for him to return and win the championship made the stakes feel very high. Ariel may have feared failure, judgment from others, or disappointing his teammates. After all, he hadn't played for almost two months. What if he wasn't good enough or off his game?

Like Ariel, your brain can learn to fear almost anything—it may learn to fear failure, conflict, disorder, uncertainty, or a lack of control. Ariel's brain had learned to fear letting others down and facing judgment. These additional factors undoubtedly influenced his pain experience, even in the absence of physical injury.

Aside from fear of pain, what other fears might contribute to your symptoms?

Conflict

Failure

Disappointing others

Uncertainty

Social situations

Rejection

Judgment

Messiness

Lack of control

Other:

Nobody wants to fail or feel like they disappointed themselves or the people they care about. Consider a specific situation in your life that felt stressful or overwhelming.

Describe the situation:

When you think about it now, are the stakes lower than they seemed at the time? Why or why not?

If your biggest fear came true, what would have happened? How would you have handled it?

To Ariel, this game means so much. What might happen if he were to think about the worst-case scenario of losing the game? What could Ariel tell himself to make him feel calmer?

A lot of times, it's easy to help a friend when they are feeling afraid. If the roles were reversed, Ariel might genuinely tell a friend that no one will be mad at them if their team loses, that there will be more opportunities in the future, and that their teammates are excited about their return regardless of the game's outcome. It's easy to step back and see things clearly when you're not the one feeling fearful and in a high-stakes situation. But it's a lot harder to be that calm, compassionate, and reassuring friend to yourself.

Here's a technique to help lower the stakes when a fear-inducing thought pops up. Picture a news broadcaster following you around, announcing the worst-case scenario of your fears. For example, imagine you are in class, and your teacher informs you that you will be taking a pop quiz on a subject you struggle with. Worries instantly pop into your head, and the news broadcaster writes up a story with the headline "Student Fails Pop Quiz!"

Fill in your fear-inducing thought in the space at the top of this newspaper.

The PRT Times

Ask yourself, *is this a compelling headline?* Now that you see it in print, is it as alarming as it seemed when the thought was inside your head? Is this a story that everyone would want to read? Is this a story you would want to read? If not, perhaps the stakes are lower than you first anticipated. Maybe, even if your worst-case scenario comes to life, you will still be okay. Your thoughts and fears are understandable. But did you know you are much more likely to succeed in a calmer emotional state?

Imagine two classrooms are taking a math test. In one room, the teacher kindly tells the students that they are well prepared for the exam and will all do great. During the test, the room remains quiet and free of distractions. In another room, a substitute teacher constantly interrupts students to tell them how little time they have left and that they should have studied harder. Which room will produce better test results?

If your answer is the calm, quiet classroom, you are correct! Consider your inner substitute teacher. How do you speak to yourself? Is your voice calm and encouraging, or stressful and filled with pressure? The next time fear thoughts pop up, pause, communicate safety, lower the stakes (using the newspaper headline tool), and take care of yourself. You can use somatic tracking for anxiety, lean into positive sensations, or provide yourself with some compassionate self-care and reassuring messages.

YOUR PAIN STORY AND YOUR IDENTITY

Now, let's talk about your narrative or pain story. Beliefs are really powerful (remember the construction worker?). If you believe you cannot make friends, ace your math test, or heal from pain, your brain internalizes that message and limits your success. Before discussing how to change your story, let's find out where it came from.

When you face new situations, such as starting high school, entering a new social setting, or even being in pain, you develop a sense of who you are and what you are capable of. Without realizing it, you form a concept of the self. Your view of yourself is a combination of experience (things you have been through), performance (how well you did in the past), and reference (how you think people view you and how you view yourself).

What do you think about yourself when you win a sports game, ace a test, or complete something challenging?

What do you think about yourself when you lose a sports game, fail a test, or give up before completing something challenging?

These experiences and the self-talk you engage in afterward become your story or how you think about yourself. Your story includes what you believe you can handle, what you think you're good or bad at, and what you will choose to attempt or give up on.

Being in pain can add chapters to your story too. Take a moment to think about how pain impacts your story and what you believe you can handle.

What do you think about yourself when you are in pain?

What do you tell yourself when you're in pain?

____

____

What do your parents tell you when you're in pain? Your friends?

____

____

When you are in pain for a long time, it is normal to feel like there are so many things you can't do. When you have an injury like a broken ankle, your brain protects you by producing pain to prevent you from walking so that you recover. In this case, the new "story" about yourself is that there are things that you physically cannot do. In this instance, your story accurately reflects your reality.

But what if the part of your story "written" during your injury is no longer true? What if you're just stuck in that chapter? What if your pain story is preventing you from doing the things you are now capable of doing?

What situations or activities have you been avoiding?

At school: ____

How much could you try to engage with this right now?

☐ Not at all ☐ Somewhat ☐ Completely

Socially: ____

How much could you try to engage with this right now?

☐ Not at all ☐ Somewhat ☐ Completely

Extracurriculars: ____

How much could you try to engage with this right now?

☐ Not at all ☐ Somewhat ☐ Completely

When it comes to getting back to your life, it's not all or nothing. Your perceived ability may fall on a spectrum that varies throughout the day or from day to day.

ANGIE'S STORY: THE IMPACT OF SELF-TALK

Angie is a ballet dancer who looks forward to performing in *The Nutcracker* every winter. At the end of the summer, she slipped and twisted her ankle. Angie was in a lot of pain and could barely put weight on her foot. Her doctor diagnosed her with a sprained ankle that would likely heal within two to three weeks and recommended that she use a compression bandage for that healing time.

After three months, Angie still didn't feel ready to give up the bandage. She was worried about the pain and reinjuring her ankle, but she followed her doctor's directions and went to class without her bandage. As she walked into the dance studio, her mind raced with fear thoughts: "What if I haven't fully healed? What if I can't finish the class? What if I fall and humiliate myself?" As it turns out, many of her beliefs became her reality: Angie was in intense pain and left class to put on her bandage.

As December rolled around, Angie was preparing for *The Nutcracker*. Although she was excited about her role and new costume, she still worried about her injury. Before going on stage, Angie took a couple of deep breaths and told herself that she would do great, reminding herself that she knew the steps like the back of her hand. She also told herself she would be fine since she had her trusty bandage. The performance went beautifully, and she exited the stage with a huge smile.

After the show, Angie took off her ballet shoes and changed into her sweats. She gasped, realizing she had forgotten to put on her bandage in the backstage chaos—and she had danced without any pain. How was that possible?

Dancing without her bandage gave Angie new evidence about her pain. She now realized that her performance success was because of her skills and confidence and that the bandage served no other purpose than making her feel safe. When her mind drifted to scary, stressful thoughts of pain and failure before class, her pain came on. But when she gave herself empowering, confident, calming messages, she felt no pain at all. Angie had proven to herself that her ankle had healed and that she did not need a bandage to dance pain-free. Angie now had a new story about herself that led to authentic safety and released her from pain.

What does your self-talk sound like? You may have paid little attention to this before. Next time you're feeling pain, notice your inner voice. Is it kind and motivating, or does it sound more like a bully?

If you notice your self-messaging being critical and discouraging, it's time to start a new chapter and empower yourself in the face of pain. We've created the 3 C's, a three-step formula for you:

CATCH YOUR PAIN VOICE: **What is it saying you cannot do?**

CHECK IT FOR EVIDENCE: **Is this message true? How do you know? Check for evidence that lets you know if you are actually capable of trying.**

If you're not sure, conduct an experiment and give it a try!

CHANGE YOUR RESPONSE:

Intervene passively: Think of this message as a thought train entering the station. Standing on the platform, you can stay where you are, acknowledge the thought, and watch it come and go. You do not have to hop on the worry train, especially when it is inaccurate!

Intervene actively: Challenge the worry thought. This thought is a bully (often wrong and illogical), and you can confront it with an assertive and honest message based on your evidence. You can say, "That's not true; you're wrong!" and change the messaging to something more accurate. **What might you say?**

What happens when you approach your fear in this new way?

APPROACHING PAIN WITH SELF-COMPASSION

Let's try an exercise to help motivate you to intervene for yourself. Often, it's much easier to be compassionate to someone else, like a friend or a younger version of yourself.

Try to remember a time you felt hurt when you were younger. Maybe you were left out by a friend or misunderstood by a parent or teacher. Close your eyes, picture that younger self, and imagine you are watching the situation unfold before you. See if you can recall the situation, noticing the people, the environment, the sounds, and the smells.

Watch your younger self respond to what is happening and notice their emotional response. Remember, you are simply looking in and observing.

Today, what would you do for your younger self? They might be having an intense emotional response. Would you judge them harshly? What would you say? Would you try to protect them? Can you let them know that you will take care of them and are here to support them? Can you be kind, compassionate, understanding, and protective now?

Let's come back to the present. You just gathered new kind and understanding messages for your younger self. Can you direct the same messages to yourself now? Let yourself know that you've got your own back. Based on what you know about your pain, shift your self-talk to reinforce safety. Instead of self-judgment, pressure, or perfectionism, can you empower yourself by letting yourself know that you are safe and capable of handling it? You can only create new neural pathways when the pain is present, so bring it on! The pain is an opportunity to prove to your brain that your body is safe.

Shout out a couple of messages you can say to empower yourself, such as "My body is strong" or "My body has healed."

Write down some more empowerment messages here:

Know that you always have the option to approach yourself and your pain this way, the same way you would approach the younger version of yourself: with compassion, care, and reassurance.

In this chapter, you explored how your thoughts and beliefs impact the way you feel. You then discovered ways to shift your self-talk and the way you treat yourself by analyzing your pain story, checking it for accuracy, and intervening compassionately. You learned:

- How your predictions (emotional state, beliefs, memories and expectations) impact your pain
- How thoughts, beliefs, and fears raise the stakes
- How to lower the stakes
- How self-talk impacts your identity, pain, and what you think you can handle
- How to change your self-talk and intervene, either passively or actively
- How to build self-compassion and a sense of empowerment

GETTING BACK TO LIFE

You've learned about what has been reinforcing your neuroplastic pain. You've also practiced tools to rewire your brain so you can correctly interpret your sensations and choose new behaviors. You might feel apprehensive as you prepare to return to the activities or situations you have avoided.

Let's look at some beliefs that may keep you stuck in your old story, and work on getting you back to your friends, school, and activities. Even if you don't feel completely ready to go back, the only way to teach your brain that returning is safe is by doing it! This concept is the same for overcoming any fear—the only way to learn that you can swim is to gradually get into the water while using your new swimming skills. You will head back to school with a backpack filled with tools to help you overcome whatever obstacle pops up.

You might feel that if you are not completely back to your pre-pain self, it's not worth going at all. This thought is an example of all-or-nothing thinking that leads to more anxiety and avoidance.

So what can you do if you think this way or have similar tendencies like perfectionism, intensity, or people pleasing? As with pain, you may develop personality traits in response to your environment. For example, growing up in a high-achieving household may make you more conscientious and responsible. Or you may be more intense because you attend a school where being good at sports makes you more well-liked. You may even become perfectionistic simply because you like getting good grades and don't like how it feels when you don't get an A. So, your brain develops behavior patterns that make you feel you have more control over getting what you want. You might overstudy when you don't need to or miss out on hanging out with your friends to leave more time to review your notes. The decision to stay home and study is your brain overprotecting you by choosing what will make you feel calmer. But do you really end up calmer or more stressed, on edge, and lonely?

PERSONALITY TRAITS: IT'S NOT BLACK OR WHITE

Most personality traits fall along a continuum and can work for or against you depending on the intensity. You don't need to change your entire personality. No trait is all good or all bad, but let's look at specific features that may hurt you, and channel them properly to serve you better.

WORRY CONTINUUM

Worry and anxiety can help you be safe, cautious, and adequately prepared, but without limits, worry may also prevent you from enjoying the present moment.

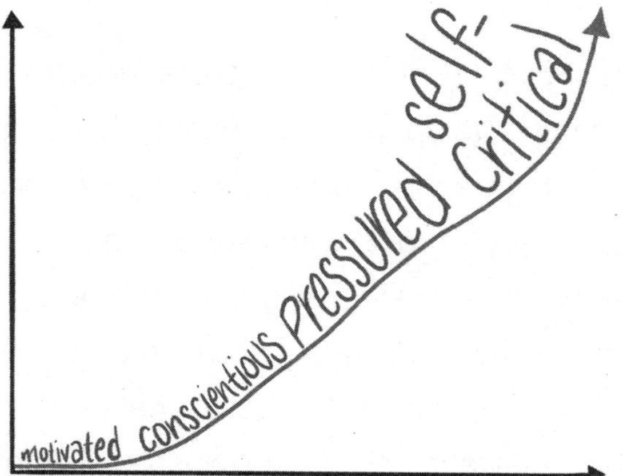

PERFECTIONISM CONTINUUM

Being motivated and conscientious may help you achieve in school. But too much pressure and perfectionism might also cause you to engage in all-or-nothing thinking, be overly self-critical, or become frozen out of fear that if it isn't perfect, it isn't worth doing at all.

PEOPLE-PLEASING CONTINUUM

Being agreeable and flexible with others may help you avoid conflict and be well liked, but it may also cause you to put your own needs last or feel taken advantage of, and prevent you from developing strong and genuine friendships.

INTENSITY CONTINUUM

Persistence may help you achieve success by helping you focus on your goal, but being hyperfocused can lead to rigidity and intensity that may cause you to be closed off to other perspectives, hindering success.

These traits can impact your mood, thoughts, beliefs, behaviors, and pain. Many of these personality traits, specifically those toward the upper-right side of the continuum, can trigger high-alert states. As you know, being in a state of high alert is connected to how your brain assesses threats. When in high-alert mode, your brain is more sensitive to anxiety, pain, and other danger signals and, as such, is more likely to interpret the world inaccurately.

Therefore, simply applying the techniques is not enough to get out of pain. Take a look at your mindset. Are you implementing techniques because you think you're supposed to (with perfectionism and rigidity)? When you struggle with a technique, are you beating yourself up (with criticism and pressure)? Remember, your brain needs authentic feelings of love, care, and safety to take you out of high-alert mode and flip off those pain signals.

Of course, we are all born with certain tendencies, but is it possible that you learned some of them? And if you did learn them, can you then unlearn them? Even if a part of your personality is predetermined, you can change some part of it by rewiring your brain.

LAUREN'S STORY: A GRADUAL RETURN

Sixteen-year-old Lauren has had chronic fatigue and back pain for the past few months. She missed a lot of school last semester because of her pain and was unable to complete many of her assignments. Lauren also struggles to get through her PE class without triggering fatigue and needing to stop halfway through. She often leaves school before PE to avoid the fear and embarrassment of sitting on the sidelines. Lauren prefers not to go at all until she can participate in the entire class perfectly.

Although Lauren used to enjoy spending time with her friends, she is terrified that almost anything could cause a pain spike, so she avoids social situations. The fear of having a bad day is overwhelming, but the longer Lauren stays away, the more awkward, uncomfortable, and less capable she feels about returning. In addition to her fear of pain, she also carries negative beliefs and worries that further contribute to her avoidance. Lauren worries she can't do well after missing so much class. She's uneasy about what her teachers will think if she turns in assignments with mistakes or does poorly on tests. She feels she is no longer smart and worries that her teachers will judge her as lazy or incompetent.

Lauren wants to get back to her life despite still having pain symptoms. She knows that her body is healthy, that her symptoms are neuroplastic, and that she has the tools necessary to embrace the activities she once loved. She's been sad and lonely and wants to be a part of things again, but has gotten used to isolating herself. The idea of being active and social has become unfamiliar. Staying away has become her comfort zone—her new default setting. When faced with pain, fatigue, or the fear of feeling pain or fatigue, Lauren goes to her safe place—isolation and avoidance—which calms her down temporarily. But by staying away, she is ultimately reinforcing that the symptoms are dangerous, keeping her from getting back to her life.

Lauren wants to reengage in her day-to-day activities, rewire her brain, and reverse that default setting to become the social, involved, and academic person she once was. She creates a fear hierarchy of the activities she has been avoiding, listing them from the least scary to the most scary so she can begin embracing them slowly. When Lauren thinks about these activities, she feels anxious about committing to any one of them, so she breaks down each fear on her list with a plan to gradually work toward that goal. After creating her plan, she feels more equipped to handle herself and less afraid of being trapped if she becomes overwhelmed.

Here's what Lauren's plan looks like:

WHAT I FEAR	WHAT I'LL DO
Doing nightly homework	1. Speak to my teacher about completing only thirty minutes of homework a night and building up the workload slowly. 2. Take breaks every thirty minutes to stretch or soothe myself as my workload increases.
Having plans with friends	1. Visit a friend's house. I'll say I can only stay for thirty minutes because I have to get home to watch my younger sister. 2. Make plans with one or two close friends at their house for one hour. When I feel ready, I'll stay longer. 3. Go to a small get-together and have my mom call with an excuse to leave after an hour. Or I can decide every thirty minutes if I want to stay a little longer.
Staying in school the full day	

As you can see, Lauren still needs a plan for gradually getting used to returning to school.

Think of some steps Lauren can take to help her with this fear, and write them down in the table above.

Now it's your turn. In the left-hand column, list the activities that you've been avoiding. Start with the least anxiety-provoking and continue to the most anxiety-provoking. On the right, write down your plan, making sure that it will enable you to take smaller, more manageable steps. You can use additional paper if you need more space.

WHAT I FEAR	WHAT I'LL DO

Creating and implementing a plan to gradually return to school, sports, or friends will help you feel more comfortable and reassured. It's okay if it takes you a little longer to move to the next step in your plan; just make sure you're moving forward and celebrating even the smallest wins. The goal is not immediately eliminating your symptoms but communicating safety and leaning into the positive regardless. Remember, your symptoms aren't reflective of damage—they are simply a misinterpretation, and you are safe!

NAVIGATING SETBACKS AND RELAPSE PREVENTION

Setbacks are inevitable. They are a part of the process. Setbacks allow you to practice your tools and build a sense of empowerment and resilience.

Frustrating things (like experiencing pain or getting a lower test score than you expected) will happen. That doesn't make the day a failure, and it doesn't make *you* a failure. A setback or disappointment doesn't take away your progress. Celebrate your wins and take breaks when you need to. Even if your symptoms pop up, that doesn't mean they are back forever. In fact, you now have proof that you can feel better and have the tools to help you respond differently.

Think about how Lauren's thinking patterns prevented her from returning to her life. When your pain pops up, do you respond similarly? Do you think the worst will happen and panic? You might get pulled into the cycle of fear and pain automatically. But everyone experiences pain at times—it's part of being human! For example, everyone gets a headache or stomach ache from time to time, but that does not mean they will be stuck in pain forever.

A pain relapse is when pain pops up after you've been feeling better for a while. A relapse might happen if you go through a stressful situation that puts your brain back on high alert, slip back into old familiar habits or thinking patterns, or get injured or think you were injured.

Slipping back into your old patterns of putting pressure on yourself, worrying about pain coming back on, or scaring yourself that the pain will never go away can feel like a reflex. Your brain does not gravitate to these scary thoughts because they are true but because they are familiar, and your brain jumps to them automatically.

A pain flare does not mean you are back at square one. All the work you have put in thus far still counts, and you can fall back on your new tools and behavioral changes. There are three stages of typical reactions to relapse. Let's talk about what to do in each stage so you can handle it and get back on track.

STAGE 1: " OH NO"

You may feel fearful, frustrated, and worried when symptoms return. You may automatically think, *Oh no, here we go again!* Instead, try to stay focused on communicating safety. At this moment, your brain needs kindness and reassurance. Messages like these can lower your brain's alert level:

It's going to be all right.

I overcame pain before, and I will do it again.

I am safe.

What soothing messages feel right to you? Write down a few ideas that you can come back to when you need them:

STAGE 2: " I'VE GOT TO GET THIS RIGHT, NOW"

You may feel pressure to use your tools immediately and perfectly, regardless of your pain intensity. But remember, when your pain is high, the best thing you can do is take care of yourself. When your pain is less intense, you can use your tools, but be sure to tune in to your mindset and energy. Are you implementing tools in a state of panic, with a desire to instantly get rid of your pain? Coming at your symptoms with intensity and pressure will only reinforce that the pain is dangerous rather than safe. Instead, remind yourself that you can turn down the intensity and increase feelings of safety, not just with the techniques but with your energy behind them. You can take breaks when necessary and use mindfulness and breathing exercises to help you access your inner calm.

STAGE 3: " OH YEAH, THIS IS WHAT I'M SUPPOSED TO DO!"

With time, you will access the same safe and easy energy you did before. Once you do that, you can use your tools properly, settle into your newly learned patterns, and activate those new neural pathways again. When you figure it out, celebrate!

MAINTAIN YOUR NEW BRAIN

Look how far you've come since starting this workbook. You learned about what kept your chronic neuroplastic pain going and how to stop fueling it. You discovered how to interpret sensations correctly and rewire your pain brain. You learned how and when to use your pain reprocessing tools to reclaim your life. But here's the thing: The pain was never the enemy. It was always your brain's way of trying to protect you. Funny as it may sound, the pain pushed you to make the changes necessary for your brain to feel safe by tuning in to your needs. But you don't need the pain anymore. To maintain your rewired brain and keep your progress going, you simply need to take care of yourself so your pain does not have to do it for you anymore!

To simplify the steps to maintaining your new brain, use the 3 R's:

RECOGNIZE: Notice when you fall back into old habits and thinking patterns that keep your brain on high alert. As you learned in chapter 7, when you are in "scary movie mode," or any one danger signal is activated, you are more likely to "jump" in the presence of another perceived threat.

REAPPRAISE: When you recognize that you are on high alert, you want to help your brain feel safe. You can challenge your thoughts, lower the stakes, look at your evidence lists, and communicate authentic safety messages.

REPLACE: Then, use the tools you have learned to increase safety. Sometimes it may be as simple as eating when you're hungry, drinking when you're thirsty, or resting when you're tired so that your brain doesn't send another danger signal like pain. And you always have your tools:

- Knowledge about neuroplastic pain and PRT
- Evidence lists
- Safety messages
- Catching fears (the 3 C's and 3 R's)
- Coloring and drawing
- Self-care menu
- Breathing exercises
- Mindfulness exercises
- Somatic tracking
- Leaning into positive sensations
- Power poses
- Lowering the stakes (the "newspaper headline" technique)
- Changing your self-talk for your empowering self-story
- Self-compassion
- Creating a fear hierarchy and making a plan for gradually managing each step
- Managing your anxiety by slowly exposing yourself to things you fear so you know you can handle them

CONCLUSION

Take a moment to celebrate all you have done. You did the hard work. Now that you know how to regulate your nervous system, handle pain triggers, and empower yourself, you have set yourself up for continued success! If you need a refresher, this workbook will always be here for you as a guide. Now that you have eliminated your fear, your pain is nothing more than a sensation. You've taken your power back and are now in charge of your brain and body. You have begun the path to staying out of pain. You're ready—we believe in you!

REFERENCES

Baliki, M., B. Petre, S. Torbey, K. Herrmann, L. Huang, T. Schnitzer, H. Fields, and A. Apkarian. 2012. "Corticostriatal Functional Connectivity Predicts Transition to Chronic Back Pain." *Nature Neuroscience* 15: 1117–1119.

Bosomtwe, S., W. Hongmei, S. Chengdong, P. Yongliang, Y. Yuzi, Z. Weiyu, and J. Zhou. 2022. "The Effects of Coloring Therapy on Patients with Generalized Anxiety Disorder." *Journal of Animal Models and Experimental Medicine* 5 (6): 502–512.

Brechet, C., L. D'Audigier, and L. Audras-Torrent. 2022. "The Use of Drawing as an Emotion Regulation Technique with Children." *Psychology of Aesthetics, Creativity, and the Arts* 16 (20): 221–232.

Burton, B., and M. F. Baxter. 2019. "The Effects of the Leisure Activity of Coloring on Post-Test Anxiety in Graduate Level Occupational Therapy Students." *Open Journal of Occupational Therapy* 7 (1): 7.

Carney, D. R., A. J. C. Cuddy, and A. J. Yap. 2010. "Power Posing: Brief Nonverbal Displays Affect Neuroendocrine Levels and Risk Tolerance." *Psychological Science* 21 (10): 1363–1368.

Drake, J. 2021. "How Drawing to Distract Improves Mood in Children." *Journal of Frontiers in Psychology* 12: 622927.

Drake, J., and E. Winner. 2013. "How Children Use Drawing to Regulate Their Emotions." *Journal of Cognition and Emotion* 27 (3): 512–520.

Fisher, J. P., D. T. Hassan, and N. O'Connor. 1995. "Minerva." *British Medical Journal* 310: 70.

Kross, E., M. G. Berman, W. Mischel, E. E. Smith, and T. D. Wager. 2011. "Social Rejection Shares Somatosensory Representations with Physical Pain." *Proceeding of the National of Science (PNAS)* 108 (15): 6270–5.

Lurie, J. M., and A. Javaid. 2024. "Visualizing Global Chronic Pain." *Anesthesia & Analgesia* 138 (4): 918–919.

Pavlov, I. P. 1927. *Conditioned Reflexes: An Investigation of the Physiological Activity of the Cerebral Cortex*. Oxford, UK: Oxford University Press.

Raja, S., D. Carr, M. Cohen, N. Finnerup, H. Flor, S. Gibson, et al. 2020. "The Revised International Association for the Study of Pain Definition of Pain: Concepts, Challenges, and Compromises." *Pain* 161 (9): 1976–1982.

Schubiner, H., W. Lowry, M. Heule, Y. K. Ashar, M. Lim, S. Mekaru, T. Kitts, and M. A. Lumley. 2023. "Application of a Clinical Approach to Diagnosing Primary Pain: Prevalence and Correlates of Primary Back and Neck Pain in a Community Physiatry Clinic." *The Journal of Pain* 25 (3): 672–681.

Siegel, D. J. 2010. *Mindsight: The New Science of Personal Transformation*. New York: Bantam Books.

Susuki, K. 2010. "Myelin: A Specialized Membrane for Cell Communication." *Nature Education* 3 (9): 59.

Woby, S. R., N. K. Roach, M. Urmston, and P. J. Watson. 2005. "Psychometric Properties of the TSK-11: A Shortened Version of the Tampa Scale for Kinesiophobia." *Pain*, 117(1-2), 137–144.

Zajonc, R. B., S. T. Murphy, and M. Inglehart. 1989. "Feeling and Facial Efference: Implications of the Vascular Theory of Emotion." *Psychological Review* 96 (3): 395–416.

DANIELLA DEUTSCH, LCSW, is cofounder, content developer, and lead trainer at the Pain Reprocessing Therapy Center, where she trains and certifies thousands of mental health clinicians and practitioners across various health disciplines. She has presented on pain treatment at international conferences and training events, and is actively involved in ongoing pain research. In addition to her work at the center, she runs a private practice—WellBody Psychotherapy—where she has guided hundreds of patients toward recovery, and leads a team of dedicated therapists and pain coaches. Daniella lives in Los Angeles, CA, with her husband and their three daughters.

PENINA ZILBERBERG, PHD, is a clinical psychologist with over twenty years of experience working with children, adolescents, and families. She specializes in treating anxiety, chronic pain, emotion regulation difficulties, impulse control disorders—and helping teens and young adults navigate key developmental transitions toward independence and self-efficacy. As a parenting expert, she provides parent training that empowers parents to foster emotional tolerance, coping skills, and confidence in their children. She has lectured on a wide range of topics related to parenting and child development, and has conducted parent and teacher workshops in local schools. Zilberberg maintains a private practice in Cedarhurst, NY.

PAULINA SOBLE, LCSW, is cofounder of the Pain Reprocessing Therapy Center, and coexecutive director of WellBody Psychotherapy. As a psychotherapist in private practice, Paulina helps patients unlearn pain by understanding their mind-body connection, and deactivating fear signals in the brain. Paulina presents at pain conferences, trainings, universities, and hospital systems, aiming to build a comprehensive network of pain reprocessing therapy (PRT) practitioners to treat the millions who suffer from chronic symptoms. Paulina spearheads the development of new initiatives, professional trainings, and educational resources to expand the reach of PRT and improve access to providers and patients.

Illustrator **ALIZA ZILBERBERG** is an art history student at Macaulay Honors College in New York, NY, with a passion for using art to foster comfort and connection. Inspired by her work with pediatric patients through her organization, Make it Home, Aliza illustrated this book to help teens navigate pain and anxiety.

Foreword writer **DAVID SCHECHTER, MD,** is a physician in Los Angeles, CA. With more than thirty-five years of experience as a family and sports medicine physician, Schechter specializes in mind-body medicine, preventive medicine, and chronic pain.

More Instant Help Books for Teens

An Imprint of New Harbinger Publications

THE CHRONIC PAIN AND ILLNESS WORKBOOK FOR TEENS

CBT and Mindfulness-Based Practices to Turn the Volume Down on Pain

9781684033522 / US $21.95

THE TRAUMA AND ADVERSITY WORKBOOK FOR TEENS

Mindfulness-Based Skills to Overcome and Recover from Prolonged Toxic Stress

9781684037971 / US $19.95

THE SELF-CONFIDENCE WORKBOOK FOR TEENS

Mindfulness Skills to Help You Overcome Social Anxiety, Be Assertive, and Believe in Yourself

9781648480492 / US $18.95

THE NEURODIVERGENCE SKILLS WORKBOOK FOR TEENS

DBT Tools to Help You Deal with Sensory Sensitivity, Manage Emotional Overwhelm, and Thrive

9781648485121 / US $21.95

THE DIALECTICAL BEHAVIOR THERAPY SKILLS WORKBOOK FOR TEENS

Simple Skills to Balance Emotions, Manage Stress, and Feel Better Now

9781648481727 / US $19.95

THE INTUITIVE EATING WORKBOOK FOR TEENS

A Non-Diet, Body Positive Approach to Building a Healthy Relationship with Food

9781684031443 / US $19.95

newharbingerpublications

1-800-748-6273 / newharbinger.com

(VISA, MC, AMEX / prices subject to change without notice)

Follow Us

Don't miss out on new books from New Harbinger.
Subscribe to our email list at **newharbinger.com/subscribe**